TASTY
PRIDE

TASTY™

PRIDE

75 RECIPES AND STORIES
FROM THE QUEER
FOOD COMMUNITY

Jesse Szewczyk

CLARKSON POTTER/PUBLISHERS
New York

Contents

To all the queer have longed to represented in food media. We restaurant, test catering compa publication. Thi stories within it is a seat at the t

cooks who
see themselves
mainstream
are in every
kitchen, hotel,
ny, studio, and
s book and the
prove that there
able for all of us.

Introduction

When I first entered culinary school in 2010, an instructor referred to one of the few openly queer students as "twinkle toes" in front of the whole class—and I was infuriated. I was mad at the teacher for singling him out. I was mad at the student for not standing up for himself. But most of all, I was mad at myself. Because even though I was a member of the LGBTQ+ community, I didn't say a word. Instead, I stood by and let it happen. And I knew that for the rest of that day, and for the rest of my time within those culinary school walls, while I was in the kitchen, I would continue to pretend to be someone I wasn't.

I had started working in restaurant kitchens as a high schooler in the Midwest several years earlier, and had run into very few cooks who looked or acted like me. At the time, I was coming to terms with my own sexuality, but was not yet ready to share it with the world. There hadn't yet been many outwardly queer chefs writing cookbooks or appearing on television, so I just assumed my culinary aspirations didn't align with my sexuality. Restaurant kitchens have historically been portrayed in media as spaces that reward cisgender, straight, white men. So, for the sake of my future career, that's the identity I committed to while in the kitchen. I was a proud gay man when I was with my friends and family, but in the kitchen I was someone else.

It wasn't until I moved to New York in 2017 and found a community of queer cooks who were loving, supportive, and—to my pleasant surprise—wildly successful that I began to publicly celebrate and embrace who I truly am, both inside the kitchen and out. Fueled by this renewed sense of confidence and pride, my professional life changed for the better. Now, as a food writer with the honor of working for Tasty, one of the largest and most recognizable food media brands in the world, I want to use my reach to showcase the talents of queer cooks. I hope to provide others with that same sense of pride I felt when I first moved to New York and witnessed my community thriving. I want to pass on the gift of finding joy in each other's successes, and thanks to Tasty's support, I am finally able to do so.

With this cookbook, I wanted to curate a collection of recipes and stories to show people like my younger self that queer professionals are thriving in the culinary industry. I wanted to present the incredible accomplishments of queer cooks, proving just how much they shape the food world. Most of the recipes in this book come from people who were complete strangers to me before the project began, and many of them are the pioneers who have paved the way for more inclusive, loving, and accepting kitchens. From Julia Turshen's comforting spaghetti and turkey meatballs (see page 81) to Ruby Tandoh's sweet and salty Fudgy Miso Brownies (page 175), these recipes illustrate the rainbow of diversity and talents within the community. Whether you're a member of the community or a supportive ally searching for mealtime inspiration, you're sure to find a recipe you'll love within these pages.

Beyond the fantastic recipes, what makes this book so special are the stories behind them—stories of love, acceptance, and pride. Along with a recipe, I asked every contributor to share how food has shaped their identity. Here are recipes that celebrate the triumphs of our community, like Bill Yosses's Dark Chocolate Mousse Cake (page 196), which graced the White House dinner table during the administration of President Barack Obama, the first president to ever voice his support for marriage equality. And here are recipes that brought relief during life's defining moments, like Amelia Rampe's Cauliflower Sandwiches (page 137), which provided comfort and support the night she and her daughter came out to each other. Shrimp and Pork Wontons (page 59) helped strengthen the bonds among Melissa King's chosen family, and Karen Akunowicz's hearty Pasta Puttanesca (page 138) charmed a new girlfriend. Food has the unique power to connect, nourish, and inspire, and that's exactly how I hope you'll feel as you cook your way through this book.

But *Tasty Pride* is not simply a cookbook; it's also an investment in our community. All the contributing cooks were paid for their recipes, and, upon the book's publication, Tasty and Penguin Random House have committed to donating $50,000 in total to GLAAD, the antidefamation organization founded by LGBTQ+ people working in the media.

Thank you to the wonderful queer cooks who made this book and its subsequent donations possible. Your stories will resonate within the hearts of many, and your recipes will bring loved ones together. And for those who feel as though they need to hide or change who they are in order to succeed in the food industry, this book is proof that you can be 100 percent authentically yourself, both inside and outside the kitchen.

WITH LOVE AND PRIDE,

Jesse Szewczyk

Contributors

Aaron Hutcherson

Alana McMillan & Sabrina Chen

Alex Koones

Amelia Rampe

Andre Springer

Andy Baraghani

Anita Lo

Anna Hieronimus & Elise Kornack

Antoni Porowski

April Anderson

Arnold Myint

Art Smith

Ben Mims

Bill Smith

Bill Yosses

Bo Durham

Brian Hart Hoffman

Bryan Petroff & Douglas Quint

Casey Elsass

Charlie Monlouis-Anderle

Deborah VanTrece & Lorraine Lane

Diana Yen

Edd Kimber

Elazar Sontag

Elizabeth Falkner

Elle Simone Scott

Eric Kim

Frances Tariga-Weshnak

Gabriella Vigoreaux

Hannah Hart

Iliana Regan

Irvin Lin

Jake Cohen

James Park

Jesse Szewczyk

Jesse Tyler Ferguson

Jessica Battilana

John Birdsall

Jonathan Melendez

Josie Smith-Malave

Julia Turshen

Justin Burke-Samson

Justin Chapple

Karen Akunowicz

Katy Smith

Kia Damon

Kristopher Edelen

Libby Willis & Bill Clark

Liz Alpern

Lukas Volger

Melissa King

Michael Marino & Jorge Moret

Natasha Case & Freya Estreller

Nik Sharma

Ollie Walleck

Orlando Soto

Pichet Ong

Preeti Mistry

Rebekah Peppler

Rick Martinez

Rita Sodi & Jody Williams

Ruby Tandoh

Ryan Alvarez & Adam Merrin

Sana Javeri Kadri

Sarah Kirnon

Sean Dooley

Susan Feniger

Ted Allen

Tiffani Faison

Vaughn Vreeland

Virginia Willis

Von Diaz

Woldy A. Reyes

Yotam Ottolenghi

Zac Young

Tools
& Equipment

The recipes in this book were written by an array of chefs with a broad range of cooking styles. Some of them work in professional kitchens and use tools you may not be familiar with. While all the recipes were designed to be easy to prepare, some of them suggest using special tools—but don't let that scare you. You can purchase most of these at your local kitchen store or order them online.

COOKIE SCOOPS

Spring-loaded cookie scoops allow you to portion dough with ease and make sure every scoop is exactly the same size (but tablespoons work just fine if you're in a pinch). Brian Hart Hoffman's recipe for Wedding Cake Cookie Sandwiches (page 200) is a great example of one that would benefit from perfect scoops.

DIGITAL SCALE

While all the recipes in this book are written using volume measures (spoons or cups), there is the occasional ingredient that is listed by weight (such as chocolate or cheese, which are sold by weight). Most of the time you can look at the packaging and eyeball the amount you need, but having a digital kitchen scale is a great way to make sure the weight of each ingredient is 100 percent accurate.

DUTCH OVEN

"Dutch oven" is just a fancy name for a heavy pot with a lid. They come in handy when making soups, braises, and sauces that cook for a long time (like the sauce for Ollie Walleck's Tagliatelle with Lamb Bolognese, page 69). Because they are enameled or plain cast iron, they are heavier than your standard metal pot, which means they have less tendency to scorch on the bottom.

FINE-MESH SIEVE

This unassuming tool is a cook's best friend. It can help you strain sauces so they're silky-smooth and remove lumps from things like cocoa powder, flour, and powdered sugar—no need to buy a sifter!

FOOD PROCESSOR

From chopping herbs and grating carrots to transforming whole nuts into flour, food processors are endlessly helpful. Many models come with several disc attachments that perform a variety of tasks, such as slicing, shredding, or puréeing. They're easy to use and can save you some serious time. Cuisinart fourteen-cup food processors are a great go-to option (and our personal favorite), but smaller eight-cup models are perfect for making individual batches of pesto or hummus.

GRILL PAN

For people living without outdoor space, grill pans are a great way to mimic the experience of grilling. Some recipes in this book provide instructions for using both an outdoor grill and a grill pan, so you can make them during any season and in any kind of space.

HIGH-SPEED BLENDER

Some recipes call for a traditional countertop blender to achieve a particular texture—and that's when schlepping a blender out of your cabinet is worth the effort. High-speed models (like Vitamix or Blendtec) make silky-smooth sauces, soups, and purées within seconds.

IMMERSION BLENDER

Small and mighty, handheld immersion blenders allow you to blend soups directly in the pot, quickly mix salad dressings, and even whip cream, all without having to retrieve a heavy machine out of your cabinet.

INSTANT-READ THERMOMETER

Instant-read thermometers take the internal temperature of whatever you're cooking within a matter of seconds. They come in handy if you're making steak, chicken, or fish and aren't completely confident it's done. Instead of cutting your protein open and peeking inside, you can just insert one of these into the thickest part. You can also use it to check the temperature of frying oil, which will come in handy if you're thinking about making Alex Koones's Everything Bagel Beignets (page 28).

MANDOLINE SLICER

A mandoline creates paper-thin slices of veggies. While you could technically use a knife, a mandoline makes the task infinitely easier. Be careful when using it, as the blades are *very* sharp. Always use the hand safety guard and work slowly.

NONSTICK BAKING MATS AND/OR PARCHMENT PAPER

If you're serious about baking, nonstick baking mats are a good investment. They're made from flexible food-grade silicone and are reusable, so you can buy one and bake on it over and over again. Parchment paper is also worth stocking up on; it's great for lining baking dishes and cake pans to make sure nothing sticks, and it can be used to line baking sheets while roasting veggies and meats, too. The best part? You can just throw away the paper after roasting and your baking sheet will be a cinch to clean.

STAND MIXER

Stand mixers can help you whip, cream, and knead with ease. In most cases, using an electric hand mixer in place of a stand mixer works just fine, but some recipes rely on the power and speed of a stand mixer to achieve a different result (like April Anderson's Blueberry Gooey Butter Cake, page 192, which uses a stand mixer to whip eggs until they're thick and ribbony). Many stand mixers also come with an array of attachments, each of which accomplishes a different task: a whisk attachment helps incorporate air into batters and frostings to make them lighter, a dough hook makes kneading a breeze, while a paddle attachment creams butter and sugar together until they're perfectly pale and fluffy.

ZESTER

Also called graters, zesters can be used to zest citrus, grate spices, shred cheese, and even shave chocolate. They are endlessly useful and produce incredibly fine shreds. Many of the recipes in this book rely on them to zest lemons and limes (like Justin Burke-Samson's Lemon Poppyseed Crinkle Cookies, page 109), but if you don't have one, you can instead use the side of a box grater with the smallest holes.

Dips, Finger Foods & Snacks

Puerto Rican–Style Pimento Cheese

VON DIAZ

MAKES 4 CUPS

8 ounces extra-sharp yellow cheddar cheese, grated (2 cups)

8 ounces sharp white cheddar cheese, grated (2 cups)

½ cup diced roasted red pepper

½ cup mayonnaise

1½ teaspoons Sazón seasoning, homemade (recipe follows) or store-bought

Chopped fresh cilantro (optional)

Crackers or celery sticks

Note: The dip will keep in the refrigerator for up to 3 days or in the freezer for up to 2 months.

In the fall of 2000, I was invited to my first queer potluck. I grew up in the suburbs of Atlanta, Georgia, in a moderately conservative household, and the consistent message I received from the world around me was that being queer was dangerous. So the invitation made me uneasy. I'd heard stories about people being followed and attacked after leaving gay clubs, and I was worried that might happen to me. But I knew my way around a potluck, as these sorts of gatherings were a part of my childhood. I walked in with a bowl of popcorn, and was immediately overcome with unprecedented freedom. The people were of every shape, color, size, and gender presentation. Until that moment, I'd had no idea such a community existed—and after that, LGBTQ+ gatherings became my safe space. The more comfortable I became, the more I wanted to share the food of my culture with my new friends, so I started making some of the Puerto Rican dishes my mom had prepared when I was growing up. This pimento cheese recipe is my homage to queer spaces and a literal fusion of my Southern home and my Boricua roots.

1. In a large bowl, add the cheeses, pepper, mayonnaise, and Sazón seasoning. Using a rubber spatula, stir everything together, folding from the outside in and mashing the cheese a bit to smooth. The dip should be homogenous in color, with flecks of pepper.

2. Scoop the dip into an airtight container and refrigerate for at least 2 hours. Garnish with cilantro, and serve with crackers or celery.

Sazón Seasoning

MAKES ABOUT ½ CUP

1 tablespoon garlic powder

1 tablespoon onion powder

1 tablespoon ground cumin

1 tablespoon ground turmeric

½ teaspoon ground black pepper

2 tablespoons kosher salt

2 tablespoons ground achiote or sweet paprika

Combine the garlic powder, onion powder, cumin, turmeric, pepper, salt, and achiote in an airtight container. Cover and shake well to incorporate. The spice mixture will keep indefinitely in an airtight container at room temperature.

Everything Bagel Beignets

ALEX KOONES

MAKES 16 BEIGNETS

2 teaspoons (1 packet) active dry yeast

2 tablespoons warm water

5 tablespoons granulated sugar

2 large egg yolks

1 large egg

½ cup lukewarm whole milk

2 teaspoons dark molasses

½ teaspoon kosher salt

3 cups all-purpose flour, plus more for dusting

8 tablespoons (1 stick) unsalted butter, room temperature

2 tablespoons brown sugar or barley malt syrup

8 cups neutral oil of choice, such as canola, for frying

Everything bagel seasoning, homemade (recipe follows) or store-bought

If there's one thing I've always known about myself, it's that I love women. My first memory of joy is of holding another girl in my arms at a slumber party. And my first memories of longing are the dreams I had of my camp counselor. For years, these memories brought about feelings of shame and confusion, fear, and anger. It wasn't until I grew old enough to seek out my people that everything started to make sense. When I stopped thinking of myself as just one person, and started thinking of myself as part of a movement. I hosted my first queer pop-up dinner in 2012: a meal that charged no entry fee, but requested you bring a beverage to share. I stayed up all night cooking. I wanted to create a space where queer people could talk to one another, and what better setting to do that than over something starchy and fried, like these fluffy beignets tossed with a savory everything bagel seasoning—a treat I would serve at one of these events. It's a fun recipe that has the ability to help people connect, unite, and find their tribe.

1. In the bowl of a stand mixer, mix the yeast, warm water, and 1 tablespoon granulated sugar with a fork. Let stand until foamy and bubbly, about 5 minutes.

2. Fit the mixer with the dough hook. To the bowl, add the egg yolks, whole egg, milk, 3 tablespoons granulated sugar, the molasses, and salt. Mix on low speed until well combined. Gradually add the flour and mix for 2 minutes, until slightly crumbly but starting to come together. Scrape down the sides of the bowl with a spatula. With the mixer running, add the butter, 1 tablespoon at a time. Continue mixing until the dough is smooth and pulls away from the sides of the bowl, 4 to 6 minutes.

3. Turn the dough out onto a lightly floured surface and knead until no longer sticky, 2 to 3 minutes. Transfer to a lightly greased bowl, cover, and let rise in a warm place until doubled in volume, about 1 hour.

4. In a large pot, combine 2 quarts of water, the brown sugar, and remaining tablespoon of granulated sugar and bring to a boil. Prepare a baking sheet by lining it with paper towels.

5. Roll out the dough to a 10-inch square rectangle about ¼ inch thick. Cut the dough into sixteen 2½-inch squares. Using a slotted spoon, dip each dough square in the boiling water bath for a few seconds on each side. Transfer to the baking sheet to dry.

6. Heat the oil in a large pot over medium heat until it reaches 350°F. Set a wire rack in a rimmed baking sheet nearby. Working in batches, fry the beignets in the hot oil, flipping once, until golden brown on both sides, about 4 minutes total. Transfer to the wire rack to drain and immediately sprinkle the everything bagel seasoning on top. Serve warm.

Everything Bagel Seasoning

MAKES ABOUT ⅓ CUP

1½ tablespoons poppy seeds

1 tablespoon black sesame seeds

1 tablespoon white sesame seeds

1 tablespoon dried minced garlic

1 tablespoon dried minced onion

2 teaspoons coarse sea salt

In a small airtight container, mix the poppy seeds, black and white sesame seeds, garlic, onion, and salt. Shake well to combine. The seasoning blend will keep for several months in the airtight container at room temperature.

TASTY PRIDE

Attea Family Banana Pepper–Feta Dip

ANITA LO

MAKES 3 CUPS

3 tablespoons olive oil

1 pound hot banana peppers, stemmed, seeded, and roughly chopped (about 2½ cups)

8 ounces feta cheese, preferably Bulgarian, brine reserved

Kosher salt and freshly ground black pepper

Pita or flatbread

For big family gatherings to serve alongside Lebanese food, my partner's family makes this wonder recipe that consists of just three ingredients—okay, five, if you count the salt and pepper. I included it as a subrecipe in my book, *Solo: A Modern Cookbook for a Party of One*, but I think it deserves a place in the spotlight, as it hits all the right notes, leading one to believe it's a lot more sophisticated than it really is. Its balance of spicy, briny, and acidic flavors will make you want to return to it again and again, slathered on a piece of pita or *markouk*, the Lebanese flatbread with which the Attea family serves the dip.

1. Heat the olive oil in a large pan over high heat. When the oil is shimmering, add the peppers. Reduce the heat to medium and cook, stirring occasionally, until wilted and slightly browned.

2. Transfer the peppers to the bowl of a food processor along with the feta. Process until smooth, adding 1 tablespoon of the reserved feta brine at a time until the mixture is spreadable. Season to taste with salt and pepper.

3. Serve the dip with fresh pita or flatbread.

Jerk-Roasted Chickpeas

KIA DAMON

SERVES 4

2 (15-ounce) cans chickpeas, drained and rinsed

3 tablespoons canola oil

½ teaspoon kosher salt

1 tablespoon dry jerk seasoning

Everything about who I was growing up, from how I dressed to how I spoke, was *very* queer—and this was before I had any awareness of my own sexuality. I was craving a space to express myself and freely be *other than*; as a consequence, I began to feel left out and distanced from my family and peers. When I finally came out as queer, that only furthered the distance, and it wasn't until I truly explored cooking that I felt like I was being seen again. Cooking and gathering has always been a foundation in my family. These are the threads that connect us, near and far. Through differences, family disputes, grievances, and celebrations, sharing food has always brought us back together. Now, as an adult, I am grateful to be weaving that thread through my chosen family and the loving community of queer and trans people of color with whom I surround myself. In the early years of building that chosen family, I would often cook for our get-togethers. This recipe, a simple snack of roasted chickpeas seasoned with warm spices, happens to be one of my personal favorites that I would bring to those gatherings. They're crunchy, golden, and easy to make.

1. Set a rack in the middle of the oven. Preheat the oven to 350°F.

2. Pat the chickpeas dry with paper towels and transfer to a large bowl with the canola oil and salt. Toss until well coated. Spread the chickpeas in an even layer on a lined baking sheet. Bake for 50 to 60 minutes, stirring often and rotating the baking sheet halfway through, until the chickpeas are crisp.

3. Remove the chickpeas from the oven and let cool on the baking sheet for 5 minutes. Transfer to a large bowl and toss with the jerk seasoning until well coated. Serve warm or at room temperature.

Garlicky White Bean Dip

CASEY ELSASS

SERVES 2

2 garlic cloves, smashed, plus 1 clove, halved

6 sprigs of fresh thyme

4 fresh sage leaves

¼ cup olive oil, plus more for brushing

1 baguette or crusty loaf of bread

1 (15.5-ounce) can cannellini beans, drained and rinsed

1 tablespoon fresh lemon juice

¼ teaspoon red pepper flakes

¼ teaspoon kosher salt

Freshly ground black pepper

In a lifetime of happy kitchen memories, some of my best and brightest are the times I've spent cooking with boyfriends. Ben was my college boyfriend, so our kitchen was lean on luxuries but rich in young love. Paul was a bartender who worked nights, and making dinner was a ritual I looked forward to all day, our chance to share support and steal kisses during the brief window in which our schedules lined up. Dio loves to fill the kitchen with Greek pop music, singing and dancing up a storm, making me cry with laughter, and whispering *S'agapó* (Greek for "I love you") in my ear. The meals are always a little beside the point, but there is a special alchemy in having the person I love most at my side that inspires some of my greatest creative cooking. One of my favorite dishes is this white bean dip, which was invented in the lean college years with Ben, but has stood the test of time as my dinner-party secret weapon. The steps make ideal work for two people—you and a lover, a partner, a best Judy, or whoever gives you love and inspiration in life right now—but is just as easily whipped up solo when your kitchen is awaiting its next muse.

1. In a medium saucepan, combine the smashed garlic, the thyme, sage, and olive oil. Heat the saucepan over low heat, swirling the pan occasionally, until the sage crisps and the garlic just starts to brown, about 15 minutes. Use tongs to transfer the prettiest sage leaf to a paper towel to drain. Remove and discard the remaining sage, thyme, and garlic, leaving the oil behind in the pan.

2. Place a medium skillet or grill pan over medium-high heat. Slice the baguette into rounds about ½ inch thick and brush both sides with olive oil. Working in batches, toast the rounds for about 1 minute, until crispy and browned, and then flip and cook for about 1 minute on the other side. As you remove the rounds, gently rub one side with the halved garlic clove. Arrange the rounds on a serving plate or small cutting board.

3. Heat the infused oil in the pan from step 1 to medium and add the cannellini beans. Sauté for about 5 minutes, stirring often, until the beans start to fall apart and become creamy. Use a wooden spoon to smash half the beans, keeping the dip a bit chunky.

4. Add the lemon juice, red pepper flakes, salt, and a generous amount of pepper to the beans. Stir to incorporate, then transfer the dip to a serving bowl. Place the fried sage leaf on top, garnish with more black pepper, and serve with the toasted bread.

Gougères
with Chives and Black Pepper

VIRGINIA WILLIS

MAKES 12 PUFFS

5 tablespoons unsalted butter

1 teaspoon kosher salt

¾ cup all-purpose flour

5 large eggs

¾ cup grated Gruyère cheese (about 2½ ounces)

1 teaspoon freshly ground black pepper

¼ cup minced fresh chives

Note: The gougères freeze beautifully. After baking, let them cool completely, then store in an airtight container in the freezer for up to 4 weeks. Warm and re-crisp them in the oven at 350°F for 5 to 7 minutes before serving.

Early in my career I was accepted to be a *stagiaire*, or unpaid apprentice, at École de Cuisine La Varenne in France. The school was founded by a woman named Anne Willan, and one of the first recipes I learned there was for gougères, a savory version of the pastry dough pâte à choux. Shortly after my arrival, an unscrupulous chef-instructor informed Anne that I was a lesbian, attempting to buy his way into her good graces with a snippet of gossip. I was furious at being outed, especially to my new boss, who was somewhat formidable, but Anne never once mentioned it, and the instructor's attempt at scandal did not in any way impact my learning or our work together. Years later, I became romantically involved with my literary agent—now my life partner—who happened to be Anne's longtime agent as well. It was important to me—to us—that Anne not discover our relationship through catty hearsay like in the past, so I met Anne for lunch and explained how my working relationship with Lisa had transformed into love. Upon hearing the news, she broke into a broad smile, patted my hand, and said in her crisp English accent, "Well done!" This recipe is an updated version of those same gougères I learned to make while studying in France—seasoned with black pepper and chives for added excitement. It's a recipe that reminds me of my journey to finding love.

1. Preheat the oven to 375°F. Line a baking sheet with parchment paper or a nonstick baking mat.

2. In a medium pot, bring ¾ cup water, the butter, and salt to a boil over high heat. Once boiling, remove the pot from the heat and add the flour. Immediately stir with a wooden spoon or rubber spatula until the flour is completely absorbed and the mixture is smooth and pulls away from the sides of the pot, about 1 minute. Return the pot to low heat and continue stirring for another 30 to 60 seconds, until the dough forms a ball.

3. Using a wooden spoon or rubber spatula, beat 4 eggs into the dough, one at a time, stirring until each one is fully incorporated before adding the next. Continue stirring until the dough is thick and glossy. Add the grated cheese, black pepper, and chives, and stir until thoroughly combined.

4. Transfer the batter to a piping bag fitted with a round tip or to a zippered plastic bag with a ½-inch opening cut off one corner. If using parchment, pipe 4 small dots of batter on the corners of the baking sheet to help glue it down. Pipe 12 mounds of dough about 2 inches in diameter onto the baking sheet, spacing at least 2 inches apart. Beat the remaining egg in a small bowl, then brush over the dough mounds. Dip a fingertip in the egg wash and gently press down any points. Bake until the gougères are puffed and lightly browned, about 25 minutes. Let the puffs cool slightly on the baking sheet, then transfer to a wire rack to continue cooling. Serve warm or at room temperature.

Sweet and Spicy Party Mix

LIBBY WILLIS & BILL CLARK

SERVES 12

Vietnamese Caramel Cereal

1 cup (2 sticks) unsalted butter

2 cups packed light brown sugar

1 teaspoon kosher salt

½ cup light corn syrup

2 tablespoons fish sauce

1 teaspoon baking soda

8 cups toasted rice cereal squares

1 tablespoon white sesame seeds

1 tablespoon black sesame seeds

Garlic Lime Cereal

6 tablespoons (¾ stick) unsalted butter, melted

2 tablespoons fresh lime juice

1 teaspoon garlic powder

1 teaspoon onion powder

8 cups toasted rice cereal squares

Party Mix

2 cups salted roasted peanuts

1 cup chopped crystallized ginger

1 (9-ounce) bag spicy cheese puffs

1 cup chopped freeze-dried mango

2 cups wasabi peas

We met several years ago working at a bakery in Brooklyn and became fast friends. After long days of cranking out cookies, cakes, and scones, somehow we'd still wanted to hang out and eat together. Pretty soon, that grew into throwing dinner parties together. We'd invite a random group of people over on a weeknight and come up with a menu that satisfied whatever we were craving at the time. Every dinner party needs a snack for guests to nibble on with their first drink, and so our get-togethers would start with a snack mix. The mix would vary—something that went with whatever we were cooking that night—but always welcomed people from the moment they walked in. This mix is spicy, sweet, and perfect for a summer Pride party. Our restaurant, MeMe's Diner in Brooklyn, was born out of these early dinner parties, welcoming anyone and everyone, and that's why your dinner at MeMe's always begins with a little bowl of cheese balls.

1. Make the caramel cereal: Preheat the oven to 200°F. Grease 2 baking sheets with nonstick cooking spray.

2. In a medium pot over medium heat, combine the butter, brown sugar, salt, and corn syrup. Bring to a boil, then cook for 5 minutes, until thickened. Remove the pot from the heat and stir in the fish sauce, then carefully stir in the baking soda—the mixture will bubble and foam somewhat vigorously.

3. Place the cereal in a large bowl and pour the caramel over; stir to coat well. Distribute the coated cereal evenly between the prepared baking sheets. Sprinkle the white and black sesame seeds on top. Bake for 1 hour, stirring every 15 to 20 minutes, until deep golden brown. Let the cereal cool completely on the pans. It will continue to harden as it cools. Break the cooled cereal into bite-sized clusters.

4. Make the garlic lime cereal: Increase the oven temperature to 325°F. Grease 2 baking sheets with nonstick spray. In a small bowl, mix the melted butter, lime juice, garlic powder, and onion powder.

5. Place the cereal in a large bowl and pour the butter mixture over; stir to coat. Distribute the cereal evenly between the prepared baking sheets. Bake for 12 to 15 minutes, stirring halfway, until toasted. Let cool completely on the pans.

6. Make the party mix: In a very large bowl, mix the caramel cereal, garlic lime cereal, peanuts, crystallized ginger, spicy cheese puffs, dried mango, and wasabi peas and toss until everything is well distributed. The party mix can be stored in an airtight container at room temperature for up to 3 days.

Fried Plantain Chips
with Lime Sour Cream and Mango Hot Sauce

SARAH KIRNON

SERVES 6

Mango Hot Sauce

2 tablespoons sunflower oil or other neutral oil

4 medium shallots, finely chopped

3 Scotch Bonnet chiles, or to taste, cored, seeded, and finely chopped (see Note)

3 garlic cloves, chopped

1 (¼-inch) piece fresh turmeric, peeled and finely chopped, or 1 teaspoon ground turmeric

¼ cup chopped fresh mango

¼ teaspoon sea salt, plus more to taste

¼ cup sugarcane vinegar or apple cider vinegar

¼ cup orange juice

Lime Sour Cream

1 cup sour cream

½ teaspoon lime zest

1 tablespoon fresh lime juice

1 teaspoon sea salt

Plantains

Vegetable oil, for frying

6 green plantains

Sea salt and freshly ground black pepper

My restaurant, Miss Ollie's Oakland, has become a staple in the area for many reasons. But the reason that resonates with me the most is that it is a safe space for young, brown, queer folks to hang out with their friends, loved ones, and other members of the LGBTQ+ community. Sharing a bowl of sweet plantain chips is a simple way of bringing people together, helping them to connect and bond. This recipe pairs the chips with homemade hot sauce and a cooling lime sour cream, but each is delicious all by itself. Sometimes it's the little things that let us know we are loved, like enjoying warm plantain chips with friends.

1. Make the mango hot sauce: Heat the oil in a medium pan over low heat. Add the shallots, chiles, garlic, turmeric, and mango and sauté for 5 to 7 minutes, until the aromatics start to soften. Add the salt, vinegar, and ½ cup water. Stir to combine, then cover and simmer until the aromatics are completely softened and the liquid thickens slightly, about 10 minutes.

2. Transfer the mixture to a blender and blend until smooth. Stir in the orange juice and season with more salt to taste. Transfer the hot sauce to a resealable glass jar and refrigerate until ready to use. (The hot sauce will keep for up to 2 weeks.)

3. Make the lime sour cream: In a medium bowl, stir together the sour cream, lime zest and juice, and salt. Refrigerate until ready to serve.

4. Make the plantains: Fill a large Dutch oven or heavy-bottomed pot about two-thirds of the way with vegetable oil. Heat over medium heat until the oil reaches 375°F.

5. With a very sharp knife, peel the plantains, then slice lengthwise about ⅛ inch thick. Working in batches, fry the plantains in the hot oil, flipping occasionally, until golden brown on both sides, 4 to 6 minutes. Using a slotted spoon, transfer to a paper towel–lined plate to drain. Season with salt and pepper.

6. Serve the fried plantains with the mango hot sauce and lime sour cream for dipping.

Note: Scotch Bonnet chiles are packed with heat. If you are sensitive to spice, use a small amount at first and add more as desired.

Popcorn
with Roasted Almonds and Nori

ELAZAR SONTAG

MAKES ABOUT 10 CUPS

Roasted Almonds

1 cup unsalted raw
   almonds

1 tablespoon extra-virgin
   olive oil

1 teaspoon honey

1 teaspoon kosher salt

Popcorn

¼ cup nutritional yeast

1½ teaspoons kosher salt

¼ teaspoon granulated
   garlic or garlic powder

¼ teaspoon onion powder

2 tablespoons toasted
   black sesame seeds,
   plus more for garnish

2 (8 by 7-inch inch) sheets
   toasted seaweed, cut
   into ½-inch squares

⅓ cup coconut oil

⅓ cup popcorn kernels

1 tablespoon extra-virgin
   olive oil

I only went to the queer youth group for the snacks. At least that's what I told my friends in middle school. But in truth, the center was one of the only places I felt truly happy and at ease. I wanted so badly to be there, but I wasn't ready for the outside world to know me in the way everyone in that building did. And the room *was* always stacked high with snacks: bags of chocolate-covered almonds, cheesy crackers, popcorn, and anything else we'd requested. As my friends in the group went around the room sharing updates from their week, I'd pull myself from the cushy corner of the couch I'd claimed and fill a plastic cup to the brim. Even in that room, surrounded by all that love, I wasn't ready to come out or share my story. I'd pass when it was my turn to talk, throwing back handfuls of popcorn. Ten years later, surrounded by an enormously loving community, my life couldn't be gayer. But when things get tough or stressful, I think back to those youth group meetings and the calm that settled over me as I sat on that couch eating snacks. I don't quite have the sweet tooth I used to, and I'm not as big on cheesy crackers either, so I build my own snack mix. I pop the corn kernels in coconut oil, toast the almonds, and toss the still-warm mixture with sesame seeds, nutritional yeast, and spices.

1. Make the roasted almonds: Preheat the oven to 250°F. Line a baking sheet with parchment paper.

2. In a small bowl, toss the almonds with the olive oil, honey, and salt until well coated. Spread the almonds in a single layer on the prepared baking sheet. Roast until lightly fragrant and browned, 15 to 20 minutes. Remove from the oven and let cool on the baking sheet for 10 to 15 minutes.

3. Meanwhile, make the popcorn: In a small bowl, combine the nutritional yeast, salt, granulated garlic or garlic powder, onion powder, sesame seeds, and seaweed squares.

4. Add the coconut oil and popcorn to a large pot or Dutch oven, cover with a lid, and turn the heat to medium-high. Shake the pot gently as the kernels begin to pop, and continue shaking every few seconds until there are 3 to 4 seconds between each pop. When the kernels have stopped vigorously popping, in about 5 minutes, remove the pot from the heat. Transfer the popcorn to a large bowl.

5. To finish: Roughly chop the cooled almonds. It's okay if the occasional almond remains whole or slightly larger than the others. The bigger pieces will add crunch and texture.

6. Drizzle the popcorn with the olive oil and stir to coat. Add the seasonings and chopped almonds and toss well, preferably with your hands, to combine. When the popcorn has cooled slightly, pile it into a serving bowl, top with more sesame seeds, if desired, and serve.

Baked Brie
with Stone Fruit and Chiles

JOSIE SMITH-MALAVE

SERVES 8

½ cup dried apricots

½ cup orange juice

1 peach, pitted and chopped

¼ cup sugar

1 Fresno chile, cored, seeded, and thinly sliced

¼ cup fresh lemon juice

1 (8-ounce) wheel of Brie cheese

2 tablespoons honey

¼ cup torn fresh basil

1 loaf of crusty bread, sliced and toasted

This recipe is inspired by my wife Marcy's love of all things Brie. Whenever I cook at home, she likes to throw in a *Top Chef* challenge or two when making requests around her favorite foods—and I always try to do my best to accommodate. She has brought tremendous joy to my life, and the best way for me to express my appreciation and undeniable love for her is to allow my creativity with food to bring a smile to her face and warmth to her tummy. Her love of Brie has landed this recipe on the menu at my restaurant, Bubbles + Pearls. Everyone loves it as much as she does, and I get to change it seasonally, based on whatever produce is available. I like to think of that switch as one of the many compromises any couple makes when choosing marriage: swapping berries for stone fruit, or the herbs for something heartier like thyme. We make this version during the summer, but you can use tart cranberries in place of the peaches during the colder winter months. Our love is a partnership, a commitment, and a lifelong journey we get to create with every bite, and this recipe is a direct reflection of that. You can serve this with crusty bread, crackers, or sweet apple slices.

1. In a small pot over medium heat, combine the dried apricots and orange juice. Bring to a simmer, reduce the heat to low, and cook, stirring often, until the apricots have absorbed almost all the liquid, about 10 minutes. Remove the pot from the heat and let cool completely. Transfer the apricots to a cutting board and chop into small pieces.

2. In a large, non-reactive bowl, combine the chopped apricots, the peach, sugar, chile, and lemon juice. Gently stir until the sugar is almost completely dissolved. Let the mixture sit uncovered at room temperature for 1 hour.

3. Preheat the oven to 375°F.

4. Place the wheel of Brie in a small cast-iron skillet or ceramic baking dish. Strain the fruit mixture to remove any excess liquid that has pooled at the bottom of the bowl. Mound the fruit on top of the Brie, allowing excess fruit to drop down and fill the sides of the skillet. Bake until the fruit mixture starts bubbling, about 15 minutes.

5. Remove the skillet from the oven. Drizzle with the honey, garnish with the basil, and serve immediately with sliced bread for dipping.

French Onion Dip

ANDRE SPRINGER (A.K.A. SHAQUANDA)

MAKES ABOUT 3 CUPS

3 tablespoons unsalted butter

1 beef bouillon cube

3 medium yellow onions, sliced

½ cup mayonnaise

1½ cups sour cream

¼ teaspoon kosher salt

1 to 2 tablespoons hot pepper sauce

1½ tablespoons sweet relish (optional)

1 tablespoon minced fresh chives, plus more for garnish

Smoked paprika (optional)

Sliced raw vegetables, crackers, or chips

I like to relate onions back to my drag. If they were makeup, caramelized onions would be my foundation, dehydrated varieties would add a touch of highlight, and raw ones would be my lashes. A good drag performance needs layers, just like onions add layers and complexity to a recipe. Some drag performances need a venue, while others simply need a good dip to keep the party going. Dips are great for crowds—they please everyone! This dip, made with a generous amount of onions, is inspired by my love of the allium and the many layers that go into a good performance. It's savory, rich, and the perfect thing to serve at a party. It takes humble ingredients and transforms them into something worthy of a celebration.

1. Preheat the oven to 400°F.

2. Heat a large cast-iron skillet over medium-low heat. Melt the butter in the skillet and swirl to coat the bottom and sides. Remove the skillet from the heat. Add the bouillon cube and mash it with the back of a wooden spoon to dissolve in the butter. Add the onions and stir until well coated. Cover the skillet with foil and bake for 1 hour.

3. Remove the skillet from the oven, stir the onions with a wooden spoon, then cover again almost completely, leaving a ½-inch opening for steam to escape. Bake for another 45 to 60 minutes, until the onions are deeply caramelized.

4. Remove the skillet from the oven. Add 2 tablespoons water and stir the mixture to loosen any browned bits stuck to the bottom. Scrape the onions into a bowl and let cool.

5. In a medium bowl, combine the mayonnaise, sour cream, salt, hot sauce, and sweet relish, if using. Stir in the cooled onions and the chives. Refrigerate the dip until completely cooled, about 2 hours. Garnish with more chives and a sprinkle of paprika, if desired, and serve with raw vegetables, crackers, or chips.

Beef, Lamb & Pork

Spicy Korean Pork Belly (Duru Chigi)

JAMES PARK

SERVES 4

1 pound pork belly, cut into ½-inch cubes

1 teaspoon ground ginger

1 teaspoon freshly ground black pepper

2 tablespoons gochujang (Korean red pepper paste)

4 tablespoons gochugaru (Korean red pepper flakes)

2 tablespoons soy sauce

2 tablespoons mirin (sweet rice wine)

2 tablespoons honey

1 tablespoon toasted sesame oil

6 garlic cloves, minced

3 large white onions, sliced

1 tablespoon canola oil

2 to 3 scallions, trimmed and chopped

Kosher salt

Toasted sesame seeds

Cooked white rice

Butter lettuce leaves, separated

At age 13, I came to the United States from South Korea all by myself. I was going through puberty and confused about my identity, and I never felt like I could talk to any of the host families I stayed with. They didn't understand many aspects of my life—be it my high-pitched voice or my fitted jeans. After years of feeling misunderstood and moving from host to host, I finally found an American family I could open up to, the Naumanns. Mrs. Naumann, who became my new mother, played a significant role in my coming of age. She never questioned my taste, and always empowered me to be authentically myself. She was the first person who ever heard me say, "I am gay." After coming out to her, I began sharing more about my life, especially during dinnertime—we would discuss things I could never talk to my Korean parents about because I have not come out to them. This spicy pork dish was the first thing I ever made for the Naumanns, and it became our new go-to dish to cook together. I thanked them for welcoming me into their family by cooking for them. It's fatty, spicy, savory, and full of flavor. Now every time I visit, I make this dish.

1. In a large bowl, season the cubed pork belly with the ginger and black pepper and massage until well coated.

2. In a small bowl, combine the gochujang, gochugaru, soy sauce, mirin, honey, sesame oil, and garlic and mix well to make the seasoning paste.

3. Add the onions and the seasoning paste to the bowl with the pork belly and massage with clean hands until the pork is evenly coated. Let marinate for 30 minutes.

4. In a large skillet, heat the canola oil over medium heat. Add two-thirds of the scallions and sauté until fragrant, about 2 minutes. Add the pork belly and sauté for 20 to 25 minutes, until cooked through and any moisture released from the onions has evaporated. Season to taste with salt.

5. Transfer the pork to a serving bowl and garnish with a sprinkling of sesame seeds and the remaining scallions. Serve with the cooked rice and offer butter lettuce leaves to make wraps.

Roasted Leg of Lamb
with Tangerine Juice and Calvados

JOHN BIRDSALL

SERVES 4 TO 6

1 small boneless leg of lamb (about 2¾ pounds)

4 teaspoons kosher salt

½ teaspoon tangerine or orange zest

¼ cup fresh tangerine or orange juice

¼ cup Calvados, Cognac, or Armagnac

3 sprigs of fresh rosemary, for basting (optional)

Note: Meat injectors are available at cookware shops everywhere. If you don't have one, prick the lamb about 6 times with the tip of a paring knife, making incisions about ½ inch deep. Add the lamb and about 3 tablespoons of the tangerine-Calvados mixture to a large zippered plastic bag. Seal the bag and press out all the air, then massage the marinade into the lamb.

I moved to San Francisco after college in the early 1980s, when AIDS was still only a lurking, unnamed thing and the spirit of liberation was high. I was searching for where I would fit in amid this capital of gayness—definitely not in the Castro, with its gym swagger, or in the hustler scene on Polk Street, or in the leather bars South of Market. Through my boyfriend, I met David. He worked at an art movie house, painted, and read more books than anyone I had ever known. David was a hardcore home cook. Once, he invited my boyfriend and me over for a dinner culled entirely from *The Alice B. Toklas Cook Book* from 1954, including something called *gigot de la clinique*: a roasted leg of mutton marinated for a week in wine and spices, and injected multiple times, from a doctor's syringe, with Cognac and orange juice. That night, David helped show me where I belonged: in the house of literary, aesthetic, and intellectual queerness—a child of Baudelaire and Rimbaud; of James Baldwin and Jean Cocteau; and especially of my culinary heroes, Richard Olney and the inimitable Miss Toklas. I've heavily adapted that recipe here, using young lamb, forgoing the marinade, and using tangerine juice and Calvados in a dedicated meat injector. Lightly caramelized and incredibly fragrant and juicy, this roast has all the charm of adult self-discovery.

1. If the lamb is already tied, remove and discard the strings to open up the meat. Season the lamb evenly with the salt on all sides. Push the lamb back into its original even, compact shape, and tie with fresh kitchen twine. Set aside at room temperature for 1 hour, or refrigerate overnight. If refrigerating, let the lamb sit at room temperature for about 1 hour before roasting so it comes to about 50°F at the center.

2. Set a rack in the center of the oven. Preheat the oven to 400°F.

3. In a small bowl, mix the tangerine zest and juice and the Calvados. Using a meat injector, inject about 3 tablespoons of the mixture evenly into the lamb in about six separate places, choosing the thickest parts of the meat. Set aside the remaining mixture.

4. Place the lamb in a rimmed non-reactive ovenproof dish small enough to fit without leaving a lot of empty space, such as a 9-inch skillet or ceramic baking dish. Roast the lamb, basting every 15 minutes with the reserved tangerine-Calvados mixture (tie the rosemary sprigs together with kitchen twine to use as a basting brush, if desired), until the internal temperature of the thickest part reaches 120°F for medium-rare, about 45 minutes total. (For medium, cook to a temperature of 128°F.)

5. Remove the lamb from the oven, tent loosely with foil, and let rest in a warm place for 15 to 20 minutes. Carve into thin slices and arrange on a platter. Drizzle with some of the roasting juices before serving.

Beef Picadillo Tacos
with Tomatillo Arbol Salsa

KATY SMITH

SERVES 8

4 dried pasilla negra chiles (about 1 ounce)

6 dried guajillo chiles (about 1 ounce)

12 medium tomatillos, husked

2 serrano chiles

2 heads of garlic, cloves separated and unpeeled

3 to 4 fresh árbol chiles, stemmed

½ cup orange juice

3 teaspoons kosher salt, plus more to taste

2 tablespoons olive oil

2 large white onions, diced, plus 1 additional, minced, for serving

1 cup diced carrots (about 2 large carrots)

2 teaspoons ground cumin

3 tablespoons balsamic vinegar

1 (14.5-ounce) can fire-roasted tomatoes

2 teaspoons sugar

2 cups diced golden potatoes (2 to 3 large potatoes)

2 to 3 jalapeños, seeded (optional) and diced

2 pounds lean ground beef

¼ cup finely chopped fresh cilantro leaves, plus more for serving

2 tablespoons apple cider vinegar

24 corn tortillas

I never had the patience to allow my mom to teach me how to cook. She tried countless times, but any attempt inevitably ended with a snarky comment from me—and a frustrated mom. But this pattern is not indicative of our relationship. When I was 27, I was in crisis: I had just realized I was gay, and had no idea how to break this news to my husband. Coming out at that age was not easy, nor was feeling like you were deeply hurting someone you had so much love for, but my mother was my rock through it all; she showed me nothing but support. Years later, I met my now-wife Tanya, an incredible Mexican American whom I thought I'd impress by showing off my knowledge of Mexican food. Little did I know that her mother, Rosalinda, is an amazing cook. I asked Tanya what dish her mother makes that is her favorite and I was determined to learn how to re-create it. I have spent years quietly watching over Rosalinda's shoulder, trying to master this dish. My Spanish isn't great, and Rosalinda's English isn't either, but we both speak food. Rosalinda shows her love and support for us through allowing me to crowd her in the kitchen the way my mother did me. I love this dish. It's simple, comforting, and warming. This version is not quite Rosalinda's, but I think it's pretty darn close.

1. Make the picadillo base: Heat a large skillet over medium-high heat. Fill a large bowl with hot water and set near the skillet.

2. While the skillet warms up, use kitchen shears to trim the stems off the dried pasilla negra and guajillo chiles. Cut down the length of one side so the chiles open up and lay flat. Working in batches, arrange the chiles in an even layer in the skillet. Toast the chiles, using a spatula to press them against the pan, just until they start to change color and become fragrant, about 30 seconds per side. Immediately transfer the chiles to the hot water bath. When all the chiles have been toasted, place a plate or bowl over the chiles in the water bath to ensure that they are fully submerged. Soak for 30 minutes, then drain.

3. Make the tomatillo salsa: Preheat the broiler on high. Line a baking sheet with foil.

4. Spread the tomatillos, serranos, and garlic cloves on the prepared baking sheet. Broil for about 2 minutes, then flip the garlic and serranos. Broil for 2 minutes more, then remove the garlic and serranos. Flip the tomatillos and continue broiling until browned and softened, 4 to 6 minutes more. Remove from the oven and let cool slightly. Peel the garlic.

5. Add the árbol chiles, orange juice, roasted serranos (remove the seeds if desired), about one-third of the roasted garlic, and 1 teaspoon of salt to a blender. Blend until smooth. Add 8 of the tomatillos and any juices that have collected. Pulse a few times until the salsa reaches your desired consistency. Transfer the salsa to a bowl to cool, then season with salt to taste. Rinse out the blender.

6. In a large pot or deep skillet, heat the olive oil over high heat. When the oil is shimmering, add the diced onions, carrots, and 2 teaspoons of salt. Cook for 2 minutes, stirring frequently, until starting to soften. Reduce the heat to medium low and let the onion caramelize, about 20 minutes.

7. Meanwhile, add the rehydrated chiles to the blender with the remaining 4 tomatillos, the cumin, remaining garlic, the balsamic vinegar, fire-roasted tomatoes, and sugar. Blend until completely smooth.

8. Add the potatoes and jalapeños to the pan with the onions and carrots and toss well to combine. Cover and cook for 5 minutes, stirring occasionally, until the potatoes start to soften. Add the ground beef and increase the heat to medium. Break up the beef with a wooden spoon or metal spatula and cook until no longer pink, about 8 minutes. Add the blended chile sauce and stir to combine, then reduce the heat to low. Simmer for 15 minutes, stirring occasionally, until the sauce thickens slightly and the flavors meld. Stir in the cilantro and apple cider vinegar and season with salt to taste.

9. To warm the tortillas, wrap in a damp paper towel and microwave for 30 seconds, or warm one at a time directly over a gas flame until slightly charred, then wrap in a kitchen towel to keep warm until ready to serve.

10. Serve the beef picadillo with the warm tortillas, tomatillo salsa, cilantro, and minced onion.

Shrimp and Pork Wontons

with Chili Sauce

MELISSA KING

SERVES 6

Wontons

8 ounces raw shrimp, peeled and deveined

8 ounces ground pork

1 teaspoon cornstarch, plus more for dusting

2 teaspoons Shaoxing rice wine

1 teaspoon grated fresh ginger

1 tablespoon kosher salt

¼ teaspoon white pepper

1 (12-ounce) package thin, square wonton wrappers made with egg

1 scallion, trimmed and thinly sliced

Crushed sesame seeds (optional)

Fried garlic (optional), homemade (see page 141) or store-bought

Chili Sauce

1 tablespoon light soy sauce

2 tablespoons black vinegar

1 teaspoon chili oil

½ teaspoon toasted sesame oil

½ teaspoon grated fresh ginger

½ teaspoon sugar

Note: To prep the wontons in advance, wrap the baking sheet in plastic wrap after forming them and freeze until solid, about 6 hours. Frozen wontons can be stored in an airtight bag for up to a month. When ready to cook, proceed from step 3.

The tradition of wrapping dumplings has always felt special to me. It's not just the act of wrapping them but also the sense of love and community that it brings. When I was young, my aunties and cousins would gather around a table to do this together—and after I grew up, it took me some time to find a new family with whom to share this tradition. When I was 22, I decided to move to San Francisco. A week before leaving, I came out to my parents— and I was able to pack with much less baggage and with all my family's love and acceptance. Once in San Francisco, I ached to find others in my community. I met a friend online and she introduced me to her network of queer friends. Meeting them was the first time I truly understood what it felt like to be accepted and safe. These friends opened my eyes to the area's LGBTQ+ community, took me to my first Pride, dined at all the restaurants I trained in, cheered me on through every episode of *Top Chef*, and comforted me through love and heartache. I found a community of people I now call family, and every so often, we gather around a table to share new stories and wrap dumplings together.

1. Make the wontons: Chop the shrimp into pea-sized pieces. Transfer the shrimp to a large bowl with the ground pork, cornstarch, rice wine, ginger, salt, pepper, and 2 tablespoons of water and mix very well.

2. Dust a baking sheet with cornstarch. Scoop 1 teaspoon of the filling into the center of a wonton wrapper. With a damp finger, moisten the edges with water, then fold the wrapper in half like a triangle, pressing out any excess air and making sure the edges are sealed well. Pull the side corners together like a tortellini, and pinch to seal. Lay on the baking sheet and cover with a kitchen towel to keep from drying out. Repeat with the remaining filling and wrappers, spacing them apart on the baking sheet so the wontons are not touching each other.

3. Bring a large pot of water to a boil.

4. Meanwhile, make the chili sauce: In a small bowl, whisk together the soy sauce, vinegar, chili oil, sesame oil, ginger, and sugar. Set aside until ready to serve.

5. Working in batches, add the wontons to the boiling water and cook for 2 to 3 minutes, until they float to the surface and the center is cooked through. Remove from the water with a spider or slotted spoon and transfer to a serving dish.

6. Toss or drizzle the wontons with the chili sauce and top with the scallions, crushed sesame seeds, and fried garlic, if using.

Beef Braciole
with Creamy Soft Polenta

ANNA HIERONIMUS & ELISE KORNACK

SERVES 4

Beef Braciole

½ cup plain breadcrumbs

4 garlic cloves, minced

½ cup grated Pecorino Romano cheese, plus more for serving

¼ cup chopped pine nuts

¼ cup golden raisins

2 tablespoons chopped fresh parsley

4 tablespoons olive oil

2 tablespoons kosher salt, plus more to taste

½ teaspoon freshly ground black pepper

1 teaspoon red pepper flakes

½ teaspoon toasted and ground fennel seeds

1 (30-ounce) flank steak

1 cup dry white wine

3½ cups tomato sauce

¼ cup fresh basil leaves, torn

Polenta

1 cup yellow cornmeal

1 cup whole milk

½ cup grated Pecorino Romano cheese

1 tablespoon unsalted butter

Kosher salt and freshly ground black pepper

This recipe will always hold a special place in my heart. I remember walking home from my new job managing a shop in the West Village, totally overwhelmed by the responsibilities it required, and eager to see Elise for a quiet night at home. When I opened the door to the apartment, a waft of roasting garlic filled my nose and I spotted lit candles and a set table. As appreciative as I was of her efforts, I was in no state to be romantic and felt I would let her down. She handed me a glass of wine and asked about my first day—I began to cry almost immediately, sharing how difficult it had been. Instead of feeling frustrated that her plans for a romantic evening had been thrown off course, she listened, encouraged, and consoled me—reassuring me that the dinner she'd made and the night she'd had in mind could wait. It was then that I knew I loved her. Hours later, after she'd helped me shake off the day, we dug into the dinner, forks in the pot of tender meat with warm tomato sauce. As comforting as Elise was to me, the dish was also to my belly. This recipe will always remind us of that night—the night Anna fell in love with Elise.

1. Preheat the oven to 350°F.

2. Make the beef: In a medium bowl, mix the breadcrumbs, garlic, Pecorino Romano, pine nuts, raisins, parsley, 2 tablespoons olive oil, the salt, black pepper, red pepper flakes, and ground fennel.

3. Lay the flank steak flat on a clean surface and cover the steak evenly with the breadcrumb mixture. Starting from a short end, roll up the steak into a cylinder. Using kitchen twine, tie the steak roll in several places to secure. Season the outside of the steak roll with more salt.

4. Heat the remaining 2 tablespoons oil in a large heavy-bottomed pot over medium-high heat. When the oil is shimmering, add the steak roll and cook, turning occasionally, until browned on all sides, about 6 minutes total. Add the wine and tomato sauce to the pot and bring to a rapid simmer.

5. Loosely cover the pot with foil and transfer to the oven. Roast until the meat is nearly tender, about 1 hour, turning the roll and basting with the sauce every 15 minutes. Remove the foil and cook for 15 minutes more, or until the beef is very tender.

6. While the braciole is cooking, make the polenta: Bring 3 cups of water to a boil in a medium pot over medium-high heat. Slowly whisk in the cornmeal and continue whisking until there are no lumps, about 2 minutes. Reduce the heat to low, cover, and simmer for 30 minutes, stirring often to make sure the polenta isn't sticking to the bottom.

7. Add the milk, Pecorino Romano, and butter to the polenta and stir until smooth. Season with salt and pepper to taste. Remove the pot from the heat and cover to keep warm until ready to serve.

8. Remove the braciole from the pot and slice with a sharp serrated knife. Serve over the polenta with the sauce spooned over, topped with basil and grated Pecorino Romano.

Chickpea and Chorizo Rigatoni
with Manchego and Smoky Breadcrumbs

GABRIELLA VIGOREAUX

SERVES 4

Kosher salt

3 tablespoons olive oil

½ teaspoon smoked pimentón (Spanish paprika)

½ cup panko breadcrumbs

8 ounces fresh chorizo, casings removed

3 garlic cloves, smashed

1 (15-ounce) can chickpeas, drained and rinsed

1½ cups tomato purée

2 large bunches of lacinato kale, stemmed and chopped

12 ounces rigatoni

3 ounces Manchego cheese, finely grated, plus more for serving

Chopped flat-leaf parsley, for garnish

As you're reading this, my girlfriend Diana and I are probably shvitzing in the kitchen, testing recipes for our future restaurant in Old San Juan, Puerto Rico. We met in the spring of 2018 in Brooklyn at Smith Canteen, the since-closed café where I hired her to be my baking assistant. By the next winter we were dating, practically living together, and had decided to move to Puerto Rico and open a restaurant together. (Keep your U-Haul jokes to yourself!) Working with your partner is interesting, but I look at it as an excuse to spend more time with her. Many of our "date nights" consist of recipe-testing for our restaurant. This pasta recipe is one of my favorites because it's the perfect mix of her Italian heritage and the Spanish flavors I grew up eating—complete with smoky paprika and savory Manchego cheese—and it's the exact kind of dish I hope to serve at our restaurant someday.

1. Bring a large pot of generously salted water to a boil over high heat.

2. Meanwhile, heat 1 tablespoon of olive oil in a small skillet over medium-high heat. When the oil is shimmering, add the smoked paprika and cook, stirring often, until fragrant, about 30 seconds. Add the breadcrumbs and a pinch of salt and cook, stirring, until toasted, about 3 minutes. Transfer the breadcrumbs to a plate lined with paper towels to drain.

3. Heat 1 tablespoon of olive oil in a Dutch oven or large heavy-bottomed pot over medium-high heat. When the oil is shimmering, add the chorizo and cook, breaking it up with a wooden spoon, until browned, 5 to 7 minutes. Transfer to a plate lined with paper towels to drain.

4. Add the remaining 1 tablespoon of olive oil and the garlic to the Dutch oven and cook until golden brown, about 2 minutes, scraping up any browned bits from the bottom of the pot. Add the chickpeas, tomato purée, and chorizo and cook until heated through. Stir in the kale and ½ teaspoon salt and cook until tender, 2 to 3 minutes.

5. Meanwhile, cook the rigatoni in the boiling water according to the package instructions, until al dente. Reserve 1 cup of the cooking water, then drain.

6. Add the cooked pasta to the pot with the chickpea and chorizo mixture, along with the Manchego cheese, and toss to combine, adding a bit of the reserved cooking water if the pasta looks dry.

7. To serve, divide the pasta among four serving bowls and top with the breadcrumbs, more cheese, and parsley.

Breakfast Burrito Potato Salad

JONATHAN MELENDEZ

SERVES 6 TO 8

2 pounds baby red potatoes, rinsed

Kosher salt

3 medium flour tortillas, cut into 2-inch strips

2 tablespoons vegetable oil

6 strips thick-cut peppered bacon, diced

4 large eggs

1 small yellow onion, diced

1 small red bell pepper, cored, seeded, and diced

1 small green bell pepper, cored, seeded, and diced

¼ teaspoon black pepper, plus more to taste

½ teaspoon granulated garlic, or more to taste

1 cup mayonnaise

½ teaspoon cayenne

¼ teaspoon hot sauce, plus more for serving

½ cup shredded cheddar or Monterey Jack cheese

4 scallions, trimmed and thinly sliced

Salsa of choice

My husband and I both share an undying love of breakfast burritos—so much so that we've made it our life's mission to try any and all of them in the greater Los Angeles area. You might even call us breakfast burrito connoisseurs; my husband sure considers himself one. Although we disagree on which one is the best, it's certainly one of the many food items that bring us closer together. And it's funny to think that it's also the one breakfast dish we always go out for, as simple as it is to prepare at home. This potato salad pays homage to both our ongoing burrito journey and one of our very first dates: we went on a picnic at a park in January—one of the many reasons why we love winters in Los Angeles—and I packed a simple spread of sandwiches, potato salad, fruit, and, of course, wine. Since then we've made a point of going on as many picnics as possible, and I always try to come up with new and interesting picnic-friendly dishes. The fact that this potato salad is made to resemble a breakfast burrito only renders it that much more special.

1. Preheat the oven to 425°F. Line 3 baking sheets, or as many as you have, with parchment paper.

2. Place the potatoes in a large pot and add enough cold water to cover by 1 inch. Season the water generously with salt. Bring to a boil over high heat, then reduce the heat to low and simmer the potatoes until just fork-tender, 20 to 25 minutes. Drain and set aside until cool enough to handle.

3. Spread the tortilla strips in an even layer on a baking sheet. Drizzle with the vegetable oil and season with salt. Toss to coat evenly. Bake until golden brown and crispy, 8 to 10 minutes. Leave the oven on.

4. Add the bacon to a cold medium skillet. Turn the heat to medium and cook, stirring often, until crispy, about 8 minutes. Using a slotted spoon, transfer the bacon to a plate lined with paper towels to drain. Reserve 6 tablespoons of the rendered bacon fat and discard the rest.

5. Meanwhile, bring a small pot of water to a boil over high heat. Using a slotted spoon, gently lower the eggs into the water. Cook for 7 minutes, then immediately transfer the eggs to an ice bath and let sit until cool enough to handle. Carefully peel the eggs and set aside.

6.   Working one at a time, gently press down on the potatoes with a flat spatula or the bottom of a measuring cup to lightly smash. Using your hands, break up the potatoes into chunks. Divide the potato pieces between the 2 remaining baking sheets, then divide the diced onion and bell pepper between them and drizzle the reserved bacon fat over the vegetables. Season with the ¼ teaspoon salt, the pepper, and garlic and toss to combine, then spread the vegetables in an even layer. Roast until the potatoes are crispy and the onions and peppers have softened, 20 to 25 minutes, tossing halfway. Remove from the oven and transfer to a large bowl. Let cool slightly.

7.   In a small bowl, whisk together the mayonnaise, cayenne, hot sauce, and a pinch of salt and pepper. Pour half of the sauce over the potato mixture, along with the cheese, half the bacon, and half the scallions. Gently toss until everything is evenly coated.

8.   Spread the remaining sauce on a large serving platter. Scoop the potato salad on top and garnish with the remaining bacon and scallions. Cut the eggs in half and arrange on top, along with the crispy tortilla strips. Serve with salsa or more hot sauce drizzled on top and alongside.

Tagliatelle with Lamb Bolognese

OLLIE WALLECK

SERVES 4

- ⅓ cup kosher salt, plus more to taste
- 2 tablespoons olive oil
- 1 pound ground lamb
- ½ cup ground or finely chopped prosciutto
- 1 teaspoon red pepper flakes
- 1 medium yellow onion, diced
- 1 fennel bulb, diced
- 3 garlic cloves, minced
- 3 sprigs of fresh rosemary
- 2 sprigs of fresh thyme
- 2 dried bay leaves
- ¾ cup tomato paste
- 2 cups dry white wine
- 1 quart chicken stock
- 1 pound dried tagliatelle or fettuccine
- 3 tablespoons unsalted butter, cold
- 1 cup grated Parmesan cheese

Growing up in northeast Ohio in the late '90s, my favorite evenings were the ones gathered around the table enjoying my mom's lamb bolognese with the company of my stepdad and three incredible siblings. Even though I've been a professional chef for nearly a decade now, my mom's execution of lamb bolognese will always be superior to mine. Although I was out as queer, I struggled then to find the language associated with being trans that would eventually set me free. My family has never faltered in showing their love and affection for me, both before and after my physical transition, and during my transition from cook to chef; they have always been a strong support network. I love this recipe because it takes time to build the layers of flavor, but once the dish is all together, it has depth without feeling heavy. It is the perfect pasta dish to create a sense of togetherness in the kitchen, and fill your house with warmth.

1. Add the salt to a large pot of water and bring to a boil over high heat, then reduce the heat to medium-low and maintain a simmer while you prepare the sauce.

2. Heat the olive oil in a large, wide pan over medium heat. When the oil is shimmering, add the lamb and cook halfway, about 8 minutes. Use a slotted spoon to transfer the lamb to a plate, leaving the rendered fat behind in the pan.

3. Add the prosciutto and red pepper flakes to the pan and cook until a good amount of fat has rendered from the prosciutto, about 2 minutes. Add the onion, fennel, garlic, rosemary, thyme, and bay leaves. Sweat the vegetables until they are softened and the herbs fall off the stems, 8 to 10 minutes. Add the tomato paste and vigorously stir to coat the vegetables. Cook until the paste is darkened and rusty in color and starts to stick to the bottom of the pan, about 3 minutes.

4. Deglaze the pan with the wine, scraping up any browned bits stuck to the bottom. Add the chicken stock and lamb, stirring only a few times. Bring to a boil, then reduce the heat to low and simmer for 25 to 30 minutes, until thickened. Discard the herb stems and bay leaves. Season with salt to taste.

5. Return the pot of water to a boil, then add the pasta. Cook according to the package instructions, until al dente. Drain the pasta, reserving ½ cup of the cooking water.

6. Add the butter and ½ cup of Parmesan cheese to the sauce and stir quickly to emulsify. Add the pasta and reserved water to the sauce, turning the noodles gently with tongs to coat. Use the tongs to twist bundles of the pasta onto serving plates and top with more Parmesan.

Fried Green Tomatoes
with Green Tomato Jam

KRISTOPHER EDELEN

SERVES 4

2 large eggs

2 tablespoons buttermilk

⅔ cup all-purpose flour

Sea salt and freshly ground black pepper

¾ cup coarse yellow cornmeal

2 medium green tomatoes, sliced (about 4 slices per tomato)

Neutral oil of choice, such as canola, for frying

6 ounces pimento cheese spread, homemade (see page 27) or store-bought

8 to 10 slices thick, pasture-raised bacon or pork belly, chopped and cooked

Green Tomato Jam (recipe follows)

Before founding my own culinary company, I worked in fine-dining restaurants. As a young cook, I worked my way through kitchens, gaining valuable skills. But as we all know, the culinary industry can traditionally be tough, and is not always welcoming to new ideas and perspectives. So as a queer black cook, I didn't always feel accepted, and sensed that I couldn't fully express myself. That's why I created my company: not only to promote my cuisine but also to create a safe space for people to express themselves if they belong to a group that's marginalized. My pop-up dinners are intended to be free of bias, criticism, conflict, and threatening conversations or ideas. This recipe for fried green tomatoes not only resonates with my childhood growing up in the Midwest but also is easy to make. It's topped with a sweet and savory green tomato jam to balance the richness of the crispy fried tomato slices and is garnished with bacon. Serving shareable recipes like this at my pop-up dinners is a simple way to create community and promote a sense of togetherness for all.

1. In a medium bowl, whisk together the eggs and buttermilk. In a separate medium bowl, mix the flour with a pinch of salt and pepper. Add the cornmeal to a third medium bowl.

2. Season the tomato slices lightly on both sides with pepper, then coat them in the flour and gently dust off any excess. Dip each slice in the egg mixture, letting any excess drip off, then coat in the cornmeal. Place on a wire rack set inside a rimmed baking sheet.

3. Fill a large, deep skillet about halfway with oil. Heat the oil over medium-high heat until it reaches 350°F. Add a few tomato slices to the hot oil, taking care not to overcrowd the pan. Fry until golden brown on both sides, about 3 minutes total. Transfer the tomatoes to a wire rack lined with paper towels to cool and crisp up. Repeat with the remaining slices, allowing the oil to return to 350°F between batches.

4. To serve, arrange the fried green tomatoes on a platter. Top each tomato with a dollop of pimento cheese spread and a few bacon crumbles. Finish with a spoonful of Green Tomato Jam.

Green Tomato Jam

MAKES 2 CUPS

2 pounds green tomatoes (4 to 6 medium tomatoes)

½ cup cane or granulated sugar

Zest and juice of 1 lemon (preferably Meyer)

1 teaspoon sea salt

¼ teaspoon freshly ground black pepper

¼ teaspoon smoked paprika

1. Bring a medium pot of water to a boil. Prepare an ice bath in a large bowl and set aside.

2. Score the bottoms of the tomatoes with an X. Add the tomatoes to the boiling water for about 3 minutes, then transfer them directly to the ice bath. Once the tomatoes are cool, peel off their skins with your hands. The skins should come off easily.

3. Roughly chop the tomatoes and transfer to a large pot. Add the sugar, lemon zest and juice, salt, pepper, and paprika. Stir to combine, then let sit for 20 minutes, until some of the liquid releases from the tomatoes.

4. Turn the heat to medium-high and bring the tomato mixture to a boil, stirring occasionally. Once boiling, reduce the heat to medium-low and simmer, stirring occasionally, to make sure the mixture is not burning or sticking to the bottom. Let the jam cook until thickened, about 1 hour. Once the mixture reaches a jamlike consistency, remove the pot from the heat.

5. Serve the jam with fried green tomatoes, or as desired. Leftover jam will keep in a glass jar in the refrigerator for up to 2 weeks.

Poultry

Ginger Garlic Turkey Bowls
with Brussels Sprout Chips

JESSE TYLER FERGUSON

SERVES 2 OR 3

8 to 10 ounces Brussels sprout leaves (from about 1 pound Brussels sprouts)

2 tablespoons extra-virgin olive oil

Kosher salt

1 tablespoon minced garlic (about 4 small cloves)

1½ tablespoons minced fresh ginger

1 pound ground turkey, preferably dark meat

¼ cup chicken stock

½ cup coconut aminos or low-sodium soy sauce

2 to 3 tablespoons Sriracha, or more to taste

2 tablespoons rice wine vinegar

1 cup shredded purple cabbage

2 scallions, trimmed and finely chopped

Cooked jasmine or cauliflower rice

Fresh lime juice or lime wedges

This dish holds a special place in my heart because I made it for my in-laws to celebrate their 50th wedding anniversary. My husband, Justin, and I were married in 2013, about a month after Proposition 8 was overturned, allowing same-sex couples to marry in the state of California. Having labored so hard for these rights brought an extra level of emotional weight to our wedding day, and blessed us with the inability to take our marriage for granted. Every union has rough days and trying times, and having role models in Justin's parents means the world to me. I can't think of anyone more qualified than a couple who have made it to their golden anniversary. Someday, Justin and I hope to be this kind of inspiration for our kids. So we celebrated Mike and Kris Mikita with this dinner. Normally I make this recipe with ground beef, but Kris doesn't eat red meat, so that evening I made it with dark ground turkey—which I actually liked better. And Justin is constantly going Paleo, so I served it with cauliflower rice. Clearly, the recipe is extremely versatile. I've made it with lettuce cups, white rice, and quinoa—but truly, it's so delicious, it can fly solo.

1. Preheat the oven to 350°F.

2. In a large bowl, drizzle the Brussels sprout leaves with 1 tablespoon of olive oil and toss to combine. Spread the leaves in an even layer on a baking sheet. Roast for 10 to 15 minutes, tossing halfway, until golden brown and crispy. Remove from the oven and sprinkle with a pinch of salt. Set aside.

3. Heat the remaining tablespoon of olive oil in a large cast-iron skillet over medium-high heat. Add the garlic and ginger and cook until fragrant, about 1 minute. Add the turkey, season with a pinch of salt, and cook, stirring occasionally, until the meat is no longer pink, about 5 minutes.

4. Add the stock, coconut aminos, Sriracha, and vinegar and stir well to combine, scraping up any browned bits from the bottom of the pan. Stir in the cabbage and cook until just wilted, another 3 to 5 minutes. Remove the pan from the heat and stir in the scallions.

5. Serve the turkey over rice and garnish with the Brussels sprout chips and a hearty squeeze of fresh lime juice.

Dry-Rub BBQ Chicken

BEN MIMS

SERVES 4

1 whole chicken
(3½–4 pounds)

2 tablespoons kosher salt

2 tablespoons dark brown
sugar

1 tablespoon sweet paprika

2 teaspoons dried oregano

2 teaspoons ground black
pepper

1½ teaspoons garlic
powder

1 teaspoon onion powder

1 teaspoon dried thyme

1 teaspoon dry mustard
powder

½ teaspoon ground cumin

¼ teaspoon cayenne

¼ teaspoon ground fennel
seeds (optional)

4 tablespoons (½ stick)
unsalted butter, melted

Sliced white bread, sweet
baked beans, and
mustardy coleslaw

I grew up in Mississippi, so barbecue was a big part of my life. There was pulled pork and beef brisket, sure, but my favorite was the barbecued chicken—complete with sweet baked beans, sharp, mustardy coleslaw, and a slice of white bread—that my local baseball team would sell each spring to raise money for the team. My boyfriend, who is also from the South, and I bonded over barbecue when we first met. For us, it's become a special meal we indulge in on occasion when we eat out, particularly on Valentine's Day, when everyone else is jockeying for a table at a white-tablecloth restaurant. Whenever we bring the tradition inside, though, I always make the closest thing I can to those baseball fundraiser chickens: a spatchcocked chicken rubbed with tons of spices like they do in Memphis. The dry rub, mixed with butter for extra richness and to help tame all the spices, has time to work its way into the skin and meat thanks to a one-hour rest in the fridge, and then again as an extra hit of crunchy flavor sprinkled on after cooking.

1. Set a wire rack on a rimmed baking sheet.

2. Working on a large cutting board, use kitchen shears to cut along each side of the chicken's backbone, then remove the backbone. Turn the chicken breast side up and press on the breast bone to flatten the chicken.

3. In a medium bowl, stir together the salt, brown sugar, paprika, oregano, pepper, garlic powder, onion powder, thyme, mustard powder, cumin, cayenne, and fennel seeds, if using. Spoon 1 tablespoon of the dry rub into a small bowl and set aside.

4. Pour the butter into the larger bowl of dry rub and stir to combine, then use your hands to rub the spiced butter all over the skin of the chicken. Transfer the chicken, skin side up, to the prepared baking sheet on top of the wire rack. Refrigerate for at least 1 hour, or overnight.

5. Preheat the oven to 425°F.

6. Roast the chicken in the oven until golden brown and crisp, and until an instant-read thermometer inserted into the breast meat reads 160°F, about 1 hour.

7. Transfer the chicken to a clean wire rack set on another rimmed baking sheet and sprinkle with the reserved dry rub. Tent loosely with foil and let stand for 15 minutes, then carve.

8. Serve the chicken hot with sliced bread, baked beans, and coleslaw alongside.

TASTY PRIDE

Spaghetti with Turkey and Ricotta Meatballs

JULIA TURSHEN

SERVES 4

4 tablespoons extra-virgin olive oil

6 garlic cloves, minced

1 (28-ounce) can crushed tomatoes

1 teaspoon kosher salt, plus more to taste

Freshly ground black pepper

½ cup fresh basil leaves, finely chopped

½ cup fresh parsley leaves, finely chopped

¾ cup whole-milk ricotta cheese

¼ cup finely grated Parmesan cheese, plus more for serving

1 pound ground turkey, room temperature

1 pound spaghetti, cooked according to package instructions

These meatballs were the first thing I ever cooked for my wife, Grace. While I can't guarantee that they will always lead to marriage, they are wonderful to cook for whomever you love. Sharing this story in my first solo cookbook, *Small Victories*, was intentional, and felt like a small (and even radical) victory. Cookbooks have an amazing power to normalize anything that has been othered. Proclaiming my love for my wife via meatballs meant that anytime anyone prepared the recipe, it was almost as if our own little Pride flag went along with it. Feel free to make a double batch and freeze the meatballs, cooked and in their sauce, in individual servings to defrost and warm up whenever you need a little comfort. I do just that so that when I'm out of town, Grace can have an easy, cozy dinner—and we can feel connected, even when we're apart. Meatballs, in other words, are one of our favorite love languages.

1. Preheat the oven to 425°F. Line a baking sheet with foil. Drizzle 2 tablespoons olive oil on the baking sheet and use your hands to rub it over the entire surface.

2. In a large saucepan or pot over medium-high heat, warm the remaining 2 tablespoons olive oil. Add 4 garlic cloves and cook, stirring, until they begin to sizzle, about 1 minute. Add the tomatoes and a very large pinch of salt and bring to a boil. Reduce the heat to low and let the sauce simmer, stirring every so often, until slightly reduced and the tomatoes have lost any tin-can taste, about 30 minutes. Season to taste with more salt and pepper.

3. Meanwhile, in a large bowl, combine the remaining 2 garlic cloves, the basil, parsley, ricotta, Parmesan, ground turkey, and 1 teaspoon salt. Mix everything with your hands until well combined. Roll the mixture into golf ball–sized meatballs; the mixture will be sticky, so wet your hands with a bit of water to help prevent the meat from sticking. Transfer the meatballs to the prepared baking sheet as you form them (it's okay if they are touching a little).

4. Bake the meatballs until lightly browned and firm to the touch, about 25 minutes.

5. Use tongs or a slotted spoon to transfer the meatballs to the simmering sauce (discard any juices and fat left on the baking sheet). Cook the meatballs in the sauce for 10 minutes (they can be left in the gently simmering sauce for up to 1 hour).

6. Serve the meatballs and sauce over the spaghetti, with extra Parmesan for sprinkling on top.

Grilled Spatchcock Chicken
with Peach-Dijon Glaze

RICK MARTINEZ

SERVES 6 TO 8

- **1 whole chicken (3½–4 pounds), backbone removed**
- **6 teaspoons kosher salt, plus more to taste**
- **1½ teaspoons freshly ground black pepper, plus more to taste**
- **1⅓ cups (13 ounces) peach preserves**
- **3 tablespoons whole-grain Dijon mustard**
- **2 tablespoons apple cider vinegar**
- **2 garlic cloves, grated**
- **⅓ cup plus 2 tablespoons extra-virgin olive oil, plus more for serving**
- **2 tablespoons fresh lemon juice**
- **2 tablespoons fresh lime juice**
- **2 tablespoons fresh orange juice**
- **1 pound mixed chicories, such as endive, escarole, radicchio, Treviso, or frisée, trimmed, leaves separated**
- **4 large ripe peaches, pitted and cut into wedges**
- **1 pint mixed small heirloom tomatoes, halved**
- **¼ cup fresh basil leaves**
- **¼ cup fresh mint leaves**
- **¼ cup fresh parsley leaves**
- **2 tablespoons chopped fresh chives**

Every year, my friends and I rent a house out at the Pines on Fire Island, off the south shore of New York's Long Island. Given the Pines' reputation for wild parties, it may be hard to believe that my favorite thing about being there is cooking outdoors for my friends and neighbors. Grilling on the deck—in a Speedo, of course—with the waves crashing on the beach behind me and the sun browning my skin is everything to me. The mere thought of this scene is what helps me get through the cold, dark New York City winters. This chicken recipe is a version of a dish I make during the summer, served over a salad of chicory and fresh herbs. I love that this dish not only looks beautiful and tastes amazing but also can be made ahead of time so I can enjoy low tea with my friends and still feed eight hungry boys who need energy to party later that night. Plus, when someone asks what you're cooking for dinner, you get to say "spatchcock"—that's always a hit on Fire Island.

1. Place the chicken skin side down on a cutting board. Use a sharp knife to score the length of the breastbone. Turn the chicken skin side up and press down on the breastbone to flatten. You should hear a crack and feel the bones give way. Season generously on both sides with 4 teaspoons of salt and 1 teaspoon of pepper. Set the chicken skin side up on a wire rack set on a rimmed baking sheet and chill in the refrigerator, uncovered, for at least 3 hours and up to 12 hours.

2. Remove the chicken from the refrigerator and let sit, uncovered, at room temperature for 1 hour before grilling.

3. In a medium saucepan over medium-low heat, combine the peach preserves, mustard, vinegar, half the garlic, and 1 teaspoon of salt. Bring to a boil and cook, stirring occasionally, until very thick and jammy, 8 to 10 minutes. Cover and keep warm until ready to glaze the chicken.

4. Prepare a grill for medium-high indirect heat (for a charcoal grill, bank the coals on one side of grill; for a gas grill, leave one or two burners off). Brush the chicken skin with 2 tablespoons of olive oil. Place the chicken skin side up on the grill over indirect heat. Cover the grill, placing the cover vent (if your grill has one) over the chicken so it draws the heat up and over the bird. Grill, rotating the chicken as needed so it browns evenly, until the skin is golden brown, 25 to 30 minutes.

5. Liberally brush the chicken, skin side only, with peach glaze, getting it into all the nooks and crannies, then cover and continue to cook until the skin is glassy and light amber, about 5 minutes more. Repeat the glazing process two more times, until the skin is lacquered and lightly charred in places and an instant-read thermometer inserted into the thickest part of the breast registers 160°F, about 10 minutes more.

6. Transfer the chicken to a cutting board and let rest for at least 10 minutes before carving into 8 pieces. Reserve the remaining glaze.

7. In a small bowl, whisk together the lemon juice, lime juice, orange juice, remaining garlic, ⅓ cup olive oil, 1 teaspoon salt, and ½ teaspoon pepper. Season with more salt to taste.

8. Toss the chicories, peaches, tomatoes, basil, mint, parsley, chives, and half the dressing together in a large bowl and season with more salt and pepper. When ready to serve, toss with the remaining dressing and a drizzle of olive oil.

9. Serve the chicken over the salad with the reserved glaze alongside.

TASTY PRIDE

Braised Chicken Legs
with Tomato and Split Peas (Gheymeh)

ANDY BARAGHANI

SERVES 4

4 bone-in, skin-on chicken legs, about 1½ pounds total

Kosher salt

2 tablespoons neutral oil of choice

1 large yellow onion, finely chopped

½ cup yellow split peas, rinsed

1 teaspoon ground turmeric

½ teaspoon ground cinnamon

¼ cup tomato paste

4 dried limes (limoo omani), pierced (see Note), or zest and juice of 2 limes

Flatbread or cooked rice

Tender herbs, such as parsley, mint, dill, cilantro, or tarragon

Note: Dried limes are simply limes that have been boiled in salt water and left in the sun to dry. Often added to soups and stews, they have a concentrated, somewhat fermented flavor. You can find them in Middle Eastern grocery stores or online. Pierce whole dried limes a few times with a paring knife before using to release more flavor and aroma. If you can't find dried limes, use fresh lime or lemon juice and zest or sumac.

One of my grandpa's favorite dishes was *gheymeh*, a type of *khoresh* (or Iranian stew) typically made with lamb or beef. The combination of cinnamon, tomato, and dried limes will always remind me of him. He was a religious man, and one of my most vivid memories of him was when I asked if he believed in marriage equality. I was around 8 or 9 years old at the time; while I wasn't fully aware of my gay identity, I knew I was attracted to the same sex. I don't remember his exact response, but I do remember feeling his disapproval. In a sense, that conversation was the first step of my coming-out process. Years later, at 18, I came out to my mother and extended family. But I never explicitly told my grandpa—I didn't feel the need to have that conversation. He was of a particular era and we had different beliefs, but I loved him greatly. He passed away in December 2018, and making gheymeh will always make me think of him. Even though we had our differences, these flavors brought us together and helped us find middle ground.

1. Pat the chicken legs dry and season with salt. Let sit at room temperature for at least 15 minutes and up to 1 hour.

2. Heat the oil in a large Dutch oven or heavy-bottomed pot over medium-high heat. When the oil is shimmering, add the chicken, working in batches if necessary, and cook, reducing the heat as needed to avoid scorching, until deep golden brown on both sides, 10 to 12 minutes total. Transfer the chicken to a plate, leaving the drippings behind in the pot.

3. Reduce the heat to medium and add the onion to the pot. Cook, stirring occasionally, until very soft and browned just around the edges, 8 to 10 minutes. Add the split peas, turmeric, and cinnamon and cook, stirring, until fragrant, about 20 seconds. Add the tomato paste and cook, stirring occasionally, until the paste begins to split and stick to the pan, about 4 minutes.

4. Add 6 cups of water and bring to a simmer. Return the chicken legs to the pot along with the dried limes. Season with salt. Reduce the heat to low and bring to a bare simmer. Partially cover the pot and cook, stirring occasionally, until the chicken is nearly falling off the bone and the juices have thickened, 60 to 80 minutes.

5. Remove the pot from the heat. Using the back of a wooden spoon, smash the dried limes against the side of the pot to release their juices. Season the stew with salt to taste.

6. Serve the stew with flatbread or over rice, along with a platter of tender herbs to eat in between each bite.

Homemade Tandoori Chicken

NIK SHARMA

SERVES 6 TO 8

6 pounds chicken drumsticks

2 cups plain yogurt

½ cup fresh lemon juice

1 cup chopped red onion

½ cup peeled and chopped beets

4 garlic cloves

1 (2-inch) piece fresh ginger, peeled and minced

1 teaspoon green cardamom pods

2 teaspoons cumin seeds

2 tablespoons ground turmeric

2 tablespoons coriander seeds

12 whole black peppercorns

1 tablespoon paprika

12 whole cloves

4 dried mild red chiles, such as Kashmiri

1½ tablespoons kosher salt

Lemon wedges

By the time I discovered I was gay, I had also discovered my loneliness, fear, and shame all rolled into a bundle that needed to be unwrapped. I had no one to confide in and I was exposed to media reports of Indian men and women mistreated simply for being queer—so I forced myself into an existence that required me to be someone I wasn't. But I wanted to be my authentic self and have the right to love and be loved for who I really was. I knew I needed to get away to do this—so I moved to America. Once there, I met men and women who were just like me, living and loving openly. Their experiences and stories gave me the strength and confidence to come out. I could finally be the free, unapologetic, happy, and best version of myself.

This tandoori chicken recipe is a true representation of my journey. Just as life's experiences shape and mold people into better versions of themselves, the marinade for this dish adds flavor and color, helping transform the bird into something brighter, more colorful, and livelier. A squeeze of lemon juice at the end gives the whole dish a pop of freshness.

1. Remove any skin from the chicken drumsticks. Rinse under cold water, then pat dry with paper towels. Using a paring knife, cut 2 deep slits across the flesh of each drumstick, then transfer to a large bowl.

2. To make the marinade, add the yogurt, lemon juice, red onion, beets, garlic, ginger, cardamom, cumin, turmeric, coriander, peppercorns, paprika, cloves, chiles, and salt to a food processor or blender. Blend until completely smooth.

3. Pour the marinade over the chicken and turn the drumsticks to coat the meat evenly. Cover the bowl with plastic wrap and allow the chicken to marinate in the refrigerator for at least 6 hours and up to overnight.

4. When ready to cook, set the racks in the upper and lower thirds of the oven. Preheat the oven to 400°F. Line 2 baking sheets with parchment paper.

5. Place the marinated drumsticks on the prepared baking sheets about 1 inch apart from each other. Spoon 1 to 2 tablespoons of the marinade over each drumstick. Bake the drumsticks for about 30 minutes, swapping racks and turning the drumsticks halfway through, until the internal temperature reaches 160°F. Turn the broiler to high. Working one baking sheet at a time, broil the chicken on the upper rack for 3 to 5 minutes, until the chicken is slightly charred. Transfer the chicken to a plate, cover with foil, and let rest for 2 to 3 minutes.

6. Squeeze the lemon wedges over the tandoori chicken and serve.

Taco Potatoes
with Spicy Ground Turkey

HANNAH HART

SERVES 4

4 large russet potatoes

1 tablespoon olive oil, plus more to taste

Kosher salt

1 medium yellow onion, diced

1 jalapeño, seeded (optional) and minced

1 pound ground turkey

1 (1-ounce) package taco seasoning

3 Roma (plum) tomatoes, seeded and diced

¼ cup chopped fresh cilantro

Juice of 1 lime

Shredded cheese, guacamole, and sour cream

What is it that makes a taco a taco? Is it defined by what's on the inside, such as the jalapeños, the ground meat, or the seasoning? Or is it the shell that holds it all together? This recipe tests and proves the idea that it is indeed what's on the inside that counts. Instead of a taco shell, this recipe shoves a traditional filling inside a potato, thereby creating a new and improved taco: a taco potato! In this day and age, we could all learn a thing or two from taco potatoes, and that is not to judge a taco by its shell. As easy as it might be to categorize people based on how they look, without doing the privileged work of getting to know them, recognize that their bodies can't label or reveal their identity, gender, or sexual orientation. It's what's on the inside that truly determines who they are. Cook this recipe and feel the liberation. Wear whatever kind of shell you want!

1. Preheat the oven to 350°F.

2. Using a fork, pierce the potatoes all over. Rub with olive oil and salt. Bake the potatoes directly on the oven rack for 1 hour, until tender.

3. Heat 1 tablespoon olive oil in a large skillet over medium-high heat. Add the onion and jalapeño, season with salt, and cook until starting to soften, about 3 minutes. Add the ground turkey, stirring with a wooden spoon to break apart. Add the taco seasoning and cook until the meat is no longer pink, 4 minutes. Add the tomatoes and cook for another 2 to 3 minutes, until the tomatoes just start to soften. Remove the pan from the heat and stir in the cilantro and lime juice.

4. Remove the potatoes from the oven and let cool slightly. Cut in half lengthwise and scoop out a bit of the centers.

5. Fill the potatoes with the turkey mixture. Top with shredded cheese, guacamole, and sour cream and serve hot.

Chicken Orzo Soup
with Lemon and Herbs

TIFFANI FAISON

SERVES 6

Chicken Broth

2 tablespoons olive oil

3 pounds chicken quarters, cut at the joints

2 teaspoons kosher salt

2 medium yellow onions, quartered

1 medium carrot, roughly chopped

4 celery stalks, roughly chopped

5 garlic cloves

3 sprigs of fresh thyme

8 cups chicken stock, homemade (recipe follows) or store-bought

1 bunch fresh parsley, torn

1 lemon, sliced into wheels

Chicken Soup

2 cups diced carrots

2 cups diced celery

2 cups diced yellow onions

2 cups uncooked orzo

1 cup fresh or frozen peas

1 tablespoon chopped fresh dill

1 tablespoon chopped fresh parsley

2 tablespoons chopped fresh chives

Kosher salt and freshly ground black pepper

Lemon juice

My wife is not a good sick person. She becomes sad and quiet, and starts to feel a little sorry for herself—but it's a sweet type of pitiful and my heart always breaks for her. She once came down with a rather bad flu, so I gathered ingredients for chicken soup while she was sleeping. This was the second time I'd ever made chicken soup from scratch—the first was for a beloved colleague who'd had lung cancer; watching her devour my impromptu soup on a frigid night was my last memory of her before she died. As I made it for the second time, fond memories of my colleague's friendship rushed into my kitchen as I reduced the broth to just the right viscosity, and I added the smallest amount of lemon juice and dill, coaxing intensity and brightness into the broth. I took even more time and care this time around, finishing the soup to nourish my wife. It was the first thing I cooked for my wife, and the last thing I cooked for a dear friend.

1. Make the broth: In a large heavy-bottomed pot, heat the olive oil over medium heat.

2. Season the chicken quarters with the salt. Working in batches, sear the chicken until deep brown on both sides, 10 to 12 minutes. Remove the chicken from the pot and set aside.

3. Add the onions, carrot, celery, garlic, and thyme to the same pot and cook until the vegetables are tender, about 12 minutes. Add the seared chicken and chicken stock and simmer for 2 hours, allowing the fat to emulsify back into the soup. Remove the pot from the heat, add the parsley and lemon, and let sit for 30 minutes.

4. Remove the chicken quarters and set aside until cool enough to handle. Pick off the meat and set aside, discarding the skin and bones.

5. Make the soup: Strain the stock, discarding the remaining solids, then return to the pot over medium-high heat and cook until reduced in volume by one-fourth, about 10 minutes. Add the diced carrots, celery, onions, and orzo. Cook over medium heat until the orzo is cooked and the vegetables are just tender, about 10 minutes. Add the peas, the chicken meat, and the dill, parsley, and chives. Season with salt, pepper, and lemon juice to taste. Serve immediately.

Homemade Chicken Stock

8 CUPS

2 pounds chicken bones and parts, rinsed

2 medium yellow onions, quartered

1 medium carrot, roughly chopped

4 celery stalks, roughly chopped

1 teaspoon black peppercorns

5 garlic cloves

3 sprigs of fresh thyme

The double-stock method used for this soup creates deep layers of chicken flavor. For the richest final product, I recommend making your own base stock from scratch.

In a large pot, combine the chicken, onions, carrot, celery, peppercorns, garlic, thyme, and 9 cups of water. Bring to a simmer over medium-high heat, then reduce the heat to low and cook for 2 hours, skimming any dark foam that rises to the top, but leaving any fat that rises. Cover, remove the pot from the heat, and let sit for another hour. Strain, discarding the solids. You should have about 8 cups total—if not, add water as needed. Set the stock aside until ready to use. Once cool, it can be kept in an airtight container in the refrigerator for up to 3 days, or in the freezer for up to 2 months.

Buttermilk Fried Chicken

ART SMITH

SERVES 4

Seasoned Brine

1 gallon cold water

1 cup kosher salt

2 teaspoons whole black peppercorns

5 sprigs of fresh rosemary

5 sprigs of fresh thyme

4 garlic cloves, crushed

2 medium shallots, halved lengthwise

4 fresh or dried bay leaves

Chicken

1 whole chicken (about 3 pounds), cut into 8 pieces

1 quart buttermilk

Rice bran oil or neutral oil of choice, for frying

3 cups all-purpose flour

3 cups self-rising flour, such as White Lily

3 tablespoons garlic powder

3 tablespoons onion powder

3 tablespoons kosher salt

¼ cup paprika

2 teaspoons cayenne

1 tablespoon dried thyme

Southern fried chicken is a beloved dish from my childhood. Whether it was to celebrate a new baby or honor someone's passing, fried chicken was always the star of our table on special occasions. My return to this dish came about when my former boss of ten years, Oprah Winfrey, requested it for her 50th birthday party in 2004. That day, all of Hollywood had the chance to enjoy it, and now fried chicken has become my most requested dish. People from U.S. presidents to Lady Gaga have had the opportunity to try it. My philosophy? Fried chicken takes no sides—it's for everyone! This version soaks the chicken in a simple brine before frying, helping it stay moist and infusing it with extra flavor.

1. Make the brine: In a medium pot over medium-high heat, combine the cold water and salt. Stir to dissolve the salt. Add the peppercorns, rosemary, thyme, garlic, shallots, and bay leaves. Remove the pot from the heat and steep for 1 hour.

2. Strain the brine into a large resealable container, discarding the solids. Let cool to room temperature, about 30 minutes.

3. Prepare the chicken: Add the chicken pieces to the brine. Cover and refrigerate for at least 12 hours and up to 24 hours.

4. Add the buttermilk to another large resealable container. Remove the chicken from the brine and transfer to the container with the buttermilk. Refrigerate for at least 4 hours, or up to 8 hours.

5. When ready to fry, fill a large heavy-bottomed pot about halfway with rice bran oil. Heat over medium-high heat until the oil reaches 325°F. Set wire racks onto 2 rimmed baking sheets.

6. In a large bowl, mix the flours, garlic powder, onion powder, salt, paprika, cayenne, and thyme. Working 2 pieces at a time, remove the chicken from the buttermilk, letting any excess drip off, and coat in the seasoned flour. Shake off any excess flour. Set on one of the two wire racks and repeat with the remaining chicken.

7. Working in batches, fry the chicken in the hot oil until golden brown and the internal temperature reaches 165°F, 10 to 13 minutes, depending on the size of the piece. Transfer to the second wire rack to drain. Let cool slightly, then serve.

Fish & Seafood

Filipino Lumpia

FRANCES TARIGA-WESHNAK

MAKES 50 LUMPIA

1 pound ground pork

8 ounces jumbo
    (21–25 count) shrimp,
    peeled and deveined,
    finely chopped

1 medium shallot, minced

1 head of garlic, minced

¼ large jicama, peeled and
    finely chopped

2 medium carrots, finely
    chopped

1 celery stalk, finely
    chopped

2 large eggs, beaten

2 tablespoons oyster sauce

2 teaspoons sugar

1 tablespoon kosher salt

1 teaspoon freshly ground
    black pepper

50 (8-inch) square spring
    roll wrappers

1 large egg yolk, beaten

Vegetable oil, for frying

Note: If you don't want to
fry them all at once, freeze
the filled lumpia in a single
layer until solid, then transfer
to a resealable bag and
store in the freezer for up
to 2 months. When ready to
enjoy, fry the lumpia directly
from frozen.

I came out at a really young age and my family wasn't always supportive of it. Around that same time, I also began helping my father in the kitchen. One task I distinctly remember is making *lumpia* with him, a type of Filipino spring roll we would prepare for parties and other large gatherings. My father taught me how to make them just like his grandma did: mix pork, shrimp, and finely cut vegetables to make the filling, roll them into spring roll wrappers, and fry them until golden and crisp. Before my father passed away, he raved about how proud he was of me and my success in my career. Now, every time I make this recipe, it makes me feel like I am back home in the kitchen with him. It's a recipe that helped my father and me find common ground and grow closer. It is dedicated to him.

1. In a large bowl, mix the pork, shrimp, shallot, garlic, jicama, carrots, celery, eggs, oyster sauce, sugar, salt, and pepper until well combined.

2. Place the spring roll wrappers on a plate and cover with a damp paper towel so they don't dry out. Working with one at a time, set a wrapper on a clean surface with corners pointing up and down, like a diamond. Brush a bit of beaten egg yolk on the top corner. Dollop about 2 tablespoons of filling in the center of the wrapper, spreading it horizontally. Fold the sides of the wrapper over the filling, then fold up the bottom and roll to seal. Place the roll on a baking sheet and cover with a kitchen towel to keep from drying out. Repeat with the remaining ingredients.

3. Fill a large pan with about 1 inch of vegetable oil. Heat over medium heat until the oil reaches 325°F. Fry the lumpia in batches, making sure not to overcrowd the pan, until golden brown, 4 to 5 minutes. Transfer to a paper towel–lined baking sheet to drain. Serve warm.

Beer-Steamed Crabs

with Spicy Vinegar Dipping Sauce and Corn Salad

SABRINA CHEN & ALANA McMILLAN

SERVES 4

Spicy Vinegar Dipping Sauce

2 medium red chiles, seeded and sliced

2 garlic cloves, chopped

Kosher salt

½ cup white wine vinegar

Corn Salad with Garlic Scallion Butter

4 ears of corn, husks on, ears soaked in cold water for 30 minutes

¼ cup olive oil

5 garlic cloves, smashed

4 tablespoons (½ stick) unsalted butter

1 bunch scallions (about 8), trimmed and chopped

Kosher salt and freshly ground black pepper

Beer-Steamed Crabs

18 ounces light beer

2 cups distilled white vinegar

20 live blue crabs, preferably male jumbo size, or 1½ pounds (16–20 count) shrimp, shell on, deveined

Old Bay seasoning

Growing up in the South, we each spent many summer afternoons gathered around a seafood boil—always with friends and family, and always with laughter and lively conversation. Years later, after we had both moved to New York City, we found that the opportunities to connect beyond surface-level conversation were surprisingly limited for lesbian and queer women. We quickly bonded over our passions for food and community—our shared experience growing up was our natural backdrop for connection—and we both had a deep desire to find others who felt the same way. This is what led us to creating JaynesBeard, our monthly supper club for queer women, a place we hope many will find their tribe and build lasting relationships. Whether it's breaking bread, breaking crab legs, or peeling shrimp, this meal bonds us. It gives us a chance to learn about one another in a way we might not otherwise take the time to do.

This recipe for steamed crabs with a punchy vinegar dipping sauce and a sweet grilled corn salad is the perfect recipe to bring people together, feast on seafood, and discover something new. If live crabs are not available, you can also use shell-on shrimp. For easier cleanup, spread the cooked crabs or shrimp out on a table lined with several layers of newspaper and dig in!

1. Make the spicy vinegar dipping sauce: In a mortar and pestle or food processor, combine the chiles, garlic, and a pinch of salt. Grind into a paste. Transfer the paste to a small bowl and add the vinegar. Stir to combine and season with more salt to taste. (The sauce is best made ahead and chilled. It will keep in an airtight container in the refrigerator for 3 to 4 days.)

2. Make the grilled corn salad: Heat a grill or grill pan over medium heat. Place the soaked corn on the heated grill for 15 minutes, turning every few minutes, until the kernels are tender. Remove from the grill and let cool slightly.

3. Meanwhile, heat the olive oil in a medium pan over medium-low heat. When the oil is shimmering, add the garlic and cook for 45 seconds, just to infuse the oil. Remove the garlic from the oil and discard or reserve for another use. Melt the butter in the pan, then transfer the butter and oil mixture to a large serving bowl. Add the scallions and toss gently to coat.

4. When the corn is cool enough to handle, remove the husks and slice the kernels from the cobs. Gently stir the corn into the garlic-scallion butter, keeping large pieces of corn intact. Season with salt and pepper to taste. Set aside until ready to serve.

5. Make the crabs: In a large pot with a steamer basket, combine the beer and vinegar, making sure the liquid doesn't rise above the steamer. Bring to a boil over medium-high heat. Place the crabs in the steamer basket, arranging them in layers. Generously season each layer with the Old Bay seasoning. Cover and steam until the crabs are bright red, 20 to 22 minutes. (If making shrimp, steam until they are bright pink and begin to curl, 7 to 9 minutes, rearranging halfway through so they cook evenly.)

6. Transfer the crabs to a baking sheet lined with newspaper. Serve with the grilled corn salad and spicy vinegar sauce for dipping.

Roasted Salmon
with Coconut Rice and Peas

CHARLIE MONLOUIS-ANDERLE

SERVES 4

1 cup dried black-eyed peas

2 cups brown rice

1 (13.5-ounce) can full-fat coconut milk

Kosher salt

4 dried bay leaves

1 medium yellow bell pepper

1 pound skinless salmon fillet

Coconut oil

1 medium red onion, diced

For Garnish

Chopped fresh culantro, cilantro, or flat-leaf parsley (see Note)

Sliced avocado

Fresh lemon or lime juice

Hot sauce

Note: Culantro is an herb with long, serrated leaves that can be found in the produce section of some international markets. If unavailable, cilantro or flat-leaf parsley can be substituted.

As a nonbinary person, I craft my self-expression from influences across a diverse genderscape. Gender expression extends beyond how we dress and groom ourselves into many different forms of self-expression, including cooking. At age 12, I became a vegetarian and began remixing my mom's recipes. It was my first attempt at asserting that I could go about things differently and still end up with something delicious. My food does not shy away from pushing boundaries or subverting expectations. It can be true to its cultural influences, while also breaking from tradition. This recipe is a perfect example of that: combining rice and peas with the deconstructed ingredients of one of my favorite Martinican recipes, *féroce d'avocat*, which literally translates to "fierce avocado." Traditionally it's made by mashing avocado with preserved salt cod and spices and served as a side or spread, but here it becomes a whole meal with fresh fish and peppers. Feel free to use any fatty fish, such as hake, in place of the salmon and mix up the garnishes based on your taste.

1. Place the peas in a large pot of water and bring to a boil, then turn off the heat and let sit for at least 1 hour and up to overnight. Drain.

2. In a medium pot, combine the rice, soaked peas, coconut milk, 2½ cups water, a couple of big pinches of salt, and the bay leaves. Bring to a boil over medium-high heat, then reduce the heat to low, cover, and simmer for about 40 minutes, or until the liquid is absorbed. Remove the bay leaves.

3. Preheat the oven to 425°F.

4. Meanwhile, blister the bell pepper on the stove-top by letting it sit directly over a medium flame, or broil in the oven until the skin is blackened in spots, about 5 minutes. Let cool slightly, then peel off the skin and chop the pepper, discarding the seeds and ribs.

5. Lay the salmon on a baking sheet. Check the salmon for bones, then rub with a bit of coconut oil and season with salt. Roast in the oven for 12 to 14 minutes, until the fish reaches your desired doneness.

6. Flake the fish apart into large pieces, then fold into the cooked rice and peas along with the chopped pepper and onion. Garnish with the culantro, avocado, lemon juice, and hot sauce.

Yucatán-Style Wrapped and Grilled Salmon

SUSAN FENIGER

SERVES 6 TO 8

½ cup (3½ ounces) achiote paste, such as La Perla

10 garlic cloves, chopped

1½ cups fresh orange juice

Juice of 2 limes

8 dried bay leaves, crumbled

2 teaspoons cumin seeds

1 teaspoon ground cinnamon

2 teaspoons dried thyme

1 teaspoon dried oregano

2 teaspoons sea salt, plus more for blanching collards

2 teaspoons freshly ground black pepper

3 pounds skin-on boneless side of salmon

2 bunches collard greens, washed and thick stems removed

2 white onions, sliced ½ inch thick

5 Roma (plum) tomatoes, sliced ½ inch thick

4 Anaheim chiles, roasted, peeled, seeded, and sliced into strips (see Note)

In the earliest days of our dating, my partner, Liz, tried to impress me by cooking dinner. The first thing I noticed was that the only items in her kitchen were an old container of dried dill, some salt and pepper, and a fridge that was practically empty. As a chef, I was horrified. On this first and only attempt to cook for me, she made salmon—sprinkling it with the dried dill and broiling it. It took every ounce of my self-control not to intervene and fix this disaster in the making. The salmon turned out completely underseasoned and overcooked, and had a strong taste of burnt dill: not exactly my favorite flavor combo. She completed the meal with a side of boiled green beans garnished with salt, and a salad served with dressing on the side. Despite the lackluster meal, she won me over and we've been together for more than two decades. When we're in the mood for salmon, we now cook up this recipe for Yucatán-style wrapped and grilled salmon inspired by my road trips to the coast of Mexico; it features the bright, bold flavors of achiote, citrus, and cinnamon. Just a little bit tastier.

1. In a medium bowl, mash together the achiote paste, garlic, orange juice, lime juice, bay leaves, cumin, cinnamon, thyme, oregano, salt, and pepper with a fork. Using a sharp knife, score several diagonal lines along the skin side of the salmon. Set the fish in a rimmed baking dish and pour the achiote marinade over, turning to coat both sides of the fish. Cover with plastic wrap and marinate in the refrigerator for 1 hour.

2. Bring a large pot of salted water to a boil. Prepare an ice bath in a large bowl and set nearby.

3. Shave the remaining collard stems with a sharp knife or vegetable peeler until the leaves are pliable. Working in batches, blanch the collards in the boiling water just until the water returns to a boil. Transfer the leaves to the ice bath to cool, then drain.

4. Preheat a grill or grill pan over medium-high heat. Line a baking sheet with a large piece of foil (you may need to overlap a few sheets). Arrange the blanched collards on the baking sheet, overlapping to form a rectangle as long as the fish and more than twice as wide.

Note: Roast fresh chiles directly over a gas flame or on a baking sheet under the broiler. Turn frequently to ensure the skin is evenly charred, without burning or drying out the flesh. Transfer the charred chiles to a plastic bag, tie the top closed, and let them steam until cool to the touch, 10 to 15 minutes. Pull off the charred skin by hand, then dip the chiles briefly in water to remove any blackened bits. Do not peel the chiles under running water, which will wash away flavorful juices. Once peeled, cut away the stems, seeds, and veins.

5. Place the marinated fish, skin side down, in the middle of the collard rectangle. Top with the onions, tomatoes, and Anaheim chiles. Wrap the collards over the fish (the dampness will make them cling), then wrap the foil around the greens. Transfer the wrapped fish to the grill. Cook for 7 to 8 minutes, then carefully lift the fish with 2 spatulas, one on each end, and gently flip over to continue cooking on the other side for another 7 to 8 minutes, until just cooked through.

6. To serve, transfer the wrapped fish to a serving platter. Remove the foil and open up the greens.

Grilled Fish "Tacos"

with Pico de Gallo, Guacamole, and Pineapple Salsa

ELIZABETH FALKNER

SERVES 4

½ cup canola oil

2 medium corn tortillas

Kosher salt

¼ cup fish sauce

2 tablespoons granulated sugar

1 cup raw cashews

½ large pineapple, cored and diced

2 jalapeños, seeded (optional) and minced, plus more, sliced, for serving

2 avocados, pitted and cubed

1 tablespoon ground cumin

2 teaspoons chipotle powder

1 bunch fresh cilantro, chopped

Juice of 1 lime

1 medium red onion, diced

4 garlic cloves, minced

3 large heirloom or beefsteak tomatoes, seeded and diced

1 bunch fresh oregano, leaves only

1 pound mahi-mahi or red snapper fillets

¼ cup extra-virgin olive oil

Freshly ground black pepper

1 head Bibb or butter lettuce, leaves separated

1 bunch fresh basil, chopped

Lime wedges

In the spring of 2015, I fell in love with a woman named Stacy who lived in Florida. She is a marathon runner, I play all kinds of sports, and we shared a love of eating bright, fresh foods together. I first made this recipe after one of her friends came back from a Florida fishing trip with some fresh mahi-mahi. We were hosting a party that evening, so I decided to make tacos with the catch. I used lettuce as the taco shells, threw some fried strips of tortilla on top for crunch, and served it with three types of salsa, including Stacy's favorite: a pineapple version with toasted cashews seasoned with fish sauce for a subtle savory kick. This topping, along with fresh herbs, gives these tacos a bit of a Vietnamese flair and makes them unique. Though Stacy and I grew apart, we still get together every now and then and make these fish tacos. This recipe will always remind me of her.

1. Preheat the oven to 325°F. Line a baking sheet with parchment paper. Heat the canola oil in a medium saucepan over medium heat until the oil reaches 325°F.

2. Cut the tortillas into thin strips about ½ inch wide and 1½ inches long. Working in batches, fry the strips in the hot oil until golden brown and crisp, about 4 minutes. Transfer with a slotted spoon to a plate lined with paper towels to drain. Sprinkle with salt.

3. In a small saucepan, combine the fish sauce, sugar, and 2 tablespoons water. Bring to a boil over medium-high heat. Add the cashews, reduce the heat to medium-low, and poach for 15 minutes.

4. Remove the cashews with a slotted spoon and spread them on the prepared baking sheet. Toast them in the oven for about 8 minutes, until golden brown.

5. Meanwhile, continue cooking the fish sauce mixture over medium heat until reduced by half, about 8 minutes. Remove from the heat and let cool. Add the pineapple, toasted cashews, and half the minced jalapeños, stirring to coat with the fish sauce caramel.

6. In a medium bowl, combine the avocados, 1 teaspoon cumin, ½ teaspoon chipotle powder, 2 tablespoons of the cilantro, and the juice of 1 lime. Mash the avocado with a fork. Season with salt to taste and set aside. In a separate medium bowl, combine the red onion, garlic, tomatoes, remaining minced jalapeño, and 2 tablespoons oregano. Season with salt to taste and set aside.

7. Heat a grill pan or large, heavy skillet over medium heat. In a large bowl, coat the mahi-mahi with the olive oil, remaining 2 teaspoons cumin, and remaining 1½ teaspoons chipotle powder. Season with

salt and pepper. Grill the fish for 2 minutes on each side, until opaque and the fish releases from the pan easily.

8. Flake the fish into large pieces and serve with the lettuce, cilantro, oregano, basil, sliced jalapeños, lime wedges, crispy tortilla strips, pico de gallo, guacamole, and pineapple salsa.

Date-Night Salmon Salad

JUSTIN CHAPPLE

SERVES 2

2 tablespoons extra-virgin olive oil

1 small red onion, half finely chopped and half thinly sliced

2 garlic cloves, minced

½ cup basmati rice, rinsed

¼ cup orzo pasta

1¼ cups chicken stock or low-sodium chicken broth

¼ teaspoon ground turmeric

Kosher salt

1 (12-ounce) center-cut salmon fillet

1 tablespoon tequila

2 teaspoons lime zest

Freshly ground black pepper

4 cups lightly packed baby arugula

1 cup lightly packed fresh cilantro leaves

2 tablespoons fresh lime juice

My affection for tequila-lime salmon began with a version I ate while sitting on a pleather couch. The couch belonged to Jason, a police officer I'd met two weeks before at the Stonewall Inn, and the salmon he cooked that night has since become the most memorable meal of my life. You see, Jason—now my husband of more than ten years—isn't the "cook" in our family, but he stole my heart with a piece of roasted salmon thoughtfully placed on a pile of rice pilaf. Even more thoughtful was the accompanying salad, which he meticulously arranged in a ring around the rim of the plate, surrounding the fish and pilaf like a halo. The memory of it makes me both laugh and cry. That meal filled me with inner peace and a sense of love that I don't think I'd felt until that moment. It offered a taste of what some might call a "normal" life—a life in which you care for someone so much that you put heartfelt effort into plating a salmon fillet. As a gay man, it was hard to visualize what my future would be, knowing I might never be able to marry. Thankfully that has since changed, but this meal reminds me it wasn't that long ago that I didn't have that right— and I don't ever want to take it for granted. My affection for this recipe began in 2003, and so did my love for the man who is now my husband.

1. Heat the olive oil in a large skillet over medium heat. When the oil is shimmering, add the chopped onion and the garlic and cook, stirring occasionally, until softened, about 5 minutes. Add the rice and orzo and cook, stirring, until the rice is translucent on the edges, about 3 minutes. Add the chicken stock, turmeric, and a generous pinch of salt. Increase the heat to high and bring to a boil. Stir once, then cover, reduce the heat to low, and simmer until the liquid is absorbed, about 20 minutes. Remove from the heat and let steam, covered, for 15 minutes. Fluff the rice with a fork, then spread on a baking sheet to cool completely.

2. Meanwhile, preheat the oven to 375°F. Line a baking sheet with foil.

3. Place the salmon skin side down on the prepared baking sheet. Brush with the tequila and sprinkle with the lime zest, then season generously with salt and pepper. Bake the salmon for about 20 minutes, until just cooked through. Let cool completely, then remove the skin and flake the salmon into 2-inch pieces; discard the skin.

4. In a large bowl, toss the cooled rice pilaf with the arugula, cilantro, lime juice, and sliced onion. Season the salad with salt and pepper. Gently fold in the salmon, then serve immediately.

Scallops
with Grilled Polenta, Bacon, and Arugula

TED ALLEN

SERVES 4

Grilled Polenta Squares

2 cups chicken broth

1 cup whole milk

2 tablespoons unsalted butter

1 cup finely ground yellow cornmeal

1 teaspoon kosher salt

Olive oil

Scallops and Arugula Salad

2 tablespoons olive oil

12 sea scallops, side muscles removed

Kosher salt

3 slices smoked cured bacon, chopped

¼ cup finely minced chives

1 garlic clove, minced

1 tablespoon fresh lemon juice

2 cups fresh arugula

1 Hass avocado, pitted and cut into large pieces

1 teaspoon champagne vinegar

Freshly ground black pepper

Food Network has always embraced LGBTQ+ people—both on-camera and in the executive suite—and I'm proud to be part of the family. Those values were also true of my first TV home on Bravo, whose original *Queer Eye for the Straight Guy* was the reason my husband and I uprooted our lives in Chicago and moved to New York City. Shortly after *Queer Eye* ended, I was judging Bravo's *Top Chef* in Miami when I first experienced shrimp and grits. This recipe is my take on the classic but made with grilled sea scallops, crispy bacon, fresh arugula, grilled polenta, and avocado assembled into a simple summer salad that's perfect for serving as a side or a main. As the Fab Five always said, *Cheers, queers!*

1. Make the polenta squares: Grease an 8-inch square baking dish with nonstick spray.

2. In a medium pot over high heat, combine the chicken broth, milk, and butter and bring to a boil. Slowly whisk in the cornmeal, then reduce the heat to low and continue whisking for about 5 minutes, until the cornmeal has thickened and all the liquid has been absorbed. Stir in the salt. Transfer the mixture to the prepared baking dish and spread in an even layer. Refrigerate for at least 2 hours or up to overnight, until set.

3. Make the scallops: Heat 1 tablespoon of olive oil in a medium skillet over medium heat. Pat the scallops dry with a paper towel and season with salt on both sides. Sear the scallops for about 4 minutes, flipping halfway, until golden brown and opaque. Transfer the scallops to a plate lined with paper towels.

4. Add the bacon to the pan and cook until brown and crispy, about 4 minutes. Transfer to a small bowl lined with paper towels to drain. Pour out all but 1 tablespoon of excess fat from the pan. Add half the chives, the garlic, and lemon juice to the pan. Cook for 2 minutes, until the chives begin to brown, then remove the pan from the heat.

5. In a medium bowl, toss the arugula with the remaining chives, avocado, remaining tablespoon olive oil, and the champagne vinegar. Season to taste with salt and pepper.

6. Heat a grill pan or griddle over medium heat. Cut the polenta into four 4-inch squares, and brush both sides with olive oil. Grill the polenta until warmed through and grill marks appear, about 3 minutes per side.

7. Arrange the polenta squares on a serving platter along with the scallops, bacon, and the arugula and avocado salad. Drizzle with the pan sauce, and season with black pepper. Serve immediately.

Grapefruit Salad
with Grilled Prawns and Thai Curried Coconut Dressing

ARNOLD MYINT (A.K.A. SUZY WONG)

SERVES 4 TO 6

Dressing

1 tablespoon Thai red curry paste

2 tablespoons fresh lime juice (about 2 limes)

2 tablespoons fish sauce

½ cup full-fat canned coconut milk

2 tablespoons dark agave nectar

Grilled Prawn Skewers

½ cup fish sauce

½ cup fresh lime juice

2 tablespoons Sriracha

2 tablespoons palm or light brown sugar

2 tablespoons minced garlic

12 head-on, tail-on prawns or large shrimp (about 2 pounds)

My mother was a tiny woman with a dynamic zest for life who loved unconditionally. Being raised in her restaurant, I watched her relationships with loyal customers—whom she called her children—grow. With my mother's recent passing, I returned to her homeland of Thailand for some soul-searching. During the trip, I found an irony in the world's perception of Thai food as simple and fast. It is actually gastronomically complex, much like my mother, who was full of color, texture, and flavor all packaged up in a beautifully humble parcel that offered a powerful surprise. My mother never judged me, my choices, my being, or my path. Many have told me how proud she was of me. She called me her Top Chef and jumped onstage when I won Miss Gay America. She was my number one fan, my friend, and a mentor with a shared passion for cooking. This dish is in my mother's honor: bright and full of flavor. The salad can be served on a large platter with lettuce leaves alongside for making wraps, if desired.

1. Submerge 12 wooden skewers in a large pan filled with room temperature water and soak for 15 to 20 minutes.

2. Meanwhile, make the dressing: In a small bowl, whisk together the curry paste, lime juice, fish sauce, coconut milk, and agave until smooth. Refrigerate until ready to use.

3. Make the prawn skewers: Combine the fish sauce, lime juice, Sriracha, sugar, and garlic in a large bowl. Add the prawns, toss to coat, and let sit for 20 minutes.

4. Heat a grill pan over medium-high heat. Thread the prawns from tail to head onto the soaked skewers and grill until the prawns are bright red and cooked through, about 5 minutes, flipping halfway through. Remove from the pan and set aside.

Salad

2 cups grapefruit segments (about 3 grapefruit)

1 cup thinly sliced green beans

1 or 2 red Fresno chiles, thinly sliced

1 cup (3 ounces) fresh bean sprouts

1 cup (3 ounces) thinly sliced red cabbage

3 ounces sunflower greens or pea shoots

1 sprig of fresh dill, fronds only, torn

8 to 10 fresh mint leaves, torn

10 to 14 fresh cilantro leaves, torn

¼ cup crispy shallots, homemade (recipe follows) or store-bought

¼ cup unsweetened shredded coconut, toasted (see Note)

¼ cup roasted peanuts

5. Make the salad: In a large bowl, combine the grapefruit segments, green beans, Fresno chiles, bean sprouts, cabbage, sunflower greens, dill, mint, cilantro, crispy shallots, coconut, and peanuts. Drizzle half the dressing over the salad and toss well, then add more dressing to taste. Top with grilled prawn skewers. The salad is best enjoyed immediately; otherwise, keep chilled until ready to serve.

Note: To toast the coconut, spread in a thin even layer in a medium pan over low heat. Cook until the bottom is lightly browned, about 7 minutes, then remove from the heat.

Crispy Shallots

MAKES ¼ CUP

¼ cup thinly sliced shallots

Kosher salt

Neutral oil, such as canola or vegetable, for frying

Cornstarch or all-purpose flour, for dusting

1. Add the shallots to a small bowl and sprinkle with salt to taste. Let sit for about 5 minutes to draw out any excess moisture. Spread the shallots on a paper towel and blot dry.

2. Fill a small pan with about ½ inch of oil and heat over medium-high heat until it reaches 350°F. Lightly dust the shallots with cornstarch. Fry them in the hot oil until golden brown and crispy, about 10 minutes. Use a slotted spoon to transfer the shallots to a paper towel–lined plate to drain.

TASTY PRIDE

Seafood Gazpacho (Cóctel de Mariscos)

BILL SMITH

SERVES 6 TO 8

1 (46-ounce) can tomato juice

1 large green bell pepper, cored, seeded, and diced

½ medium red onion, diced

1 celery stalk, diced

2 jalapeños, seeded (optional) and minced

2 ripe avocados, peeled and cubed

Zest and juice of 1 orange

1 tablespoon fresh lemon juice

2 tablespoons chopped fresh cilantro

8 ounces boiled shrimp, peeled and cut in half

8 ounces backfin crabmeat, picked over for bits of shell

12 freshly shucked oysters

1 (12-ounce) bottle orange soda (optional)

I'm a gay man who has been very fortunate to live in a progressive and diverse community. I've marched in Stonewall parades, cooked for the Chefs for Equality Dinner in Washington, D.C., and had the privilege of employing people from all walks of life in my kitchens. Because of these experiences, I have been exposed to many new recipes and techniques—like this seafood gazpacho. I've run into versions of it all over Mexico and it often appears on menus in the United States as well. It makes a terrific dinner during a week at the beach, and a wonderful appetizer when served in small portions. This is the basic recipe, but you can vary the seafood any way to suit your preferences—I've even seen it with chunks of grilled octopus. Any fish that firms up when poached will work well in this dish.

1. In a large pot or bowl, combine the tomato juice, bell pepper, onion, celery, jalapeños, avocados, orange zest and juice, and lemon juice. Stir well, then chill until very cold, at least 45 minutes, or up to 2 hours.

2. When ready to serve, gently stir the cilantro, shrimp, crab, and oysters into the soup. Ladle into bowls and top each serving with a splash of orange soda, if using.

(Mostly) Vegetarian

Black Bean Fajita Soup

AARON HUTCHERSON

SERVES 4

2 cups vegetable broth

2 (15.5-ounce) cans black beans, drained and rinsed

2 tablespoons olive oil

2 bell peppers of any color, cored, seeded, and diced

1 small red onion, diced

1 teaspoon chili powder

1 teaspoon ground cumin

Kosher salt and freshly ground black pepper

2 garlic cloves, minced

1 (14.5-ounce) can diced fire-roasted tomatoes

Fresh cilantro, lime wedges, shredded cheese, diced avocado, or sour cream

Note: If you are vegan, this soup is also for you! Just skip the sour cream and cheese on top.

In my vision of loving others, food has always played a big role—be it sharing a pepperoni pizza during a quiet evening or cooking a nice steak dinner to romance a cute boy. However, I could do neither of these things with my first boyfriend because of one inconvenient character trait: he was a vegetarian. With food playing such a big role in my life, I questioned how the relationship would work. Cooking for others is one of my love languages, yet I felt as if my vocabulary were being restricted. I wanted to cook for him but didn't know what to make. He was worth trying to figure it out for. After racking my brain, I settled on a meal of pepper and onion fajitas with all the fixings, along with black beans and rice. This soup is my homage to that meal—complete with all the vibrant garnishes that made it so delicious—but in an easy-to-make soup that is as comforting as it is flavorful.

1. Add the vegetable broth and 1 cup of black beans to a blender and blend until smooth.

2. Heat the olive oil in a large pot over medium heat. Add the bell peppers, onion, chili powder, cumin, and salt and pepper to taste, and cook, stirring occasionally, until the vegetables start to soften, about 5 minutes. Add the garlic and cook for 1 to 2 minutes more, until fragrant.

3. Add the tomatoes, remaining whole black beans, and bean purée to the pot. Bring to a boil, then reduce the heat to low and simmer, stirring occasionally, until the soup thickens slightly, 10 to 15 minutes. Season with salt and pepper. You can either leave the soup as it is, or purée with an immersion blender for a smoother consistency.

4. Ladle the soup into bowls and serve with your desired toppings.

Roasted Seaweed Risotto
with Peas

ERIC KIM

SERVES 4

6 cups unsalted vegetable broth

2 tablespoons unsalted butter

2 medium shallots, minced

1 cup Arborio or Carnaroli rice

½ cup sake

Pinch of celery seeds (optional)

2 (5-gram) packets of roasted seaweed snacks, crushed with your hands

½ cup frozen peas

1 tablespoon toasted sesame oil

½ teaspoon kosher salt, plus more to taste

Preparing a risotto takes time; there's no doubt about that. It's a deep commitment to spend half an hour standing in front of the stove. There is no greater act of love than stirring risotto for another human being—which is why when I'm in a serious relationship, I make risotto. The guys probably don't realize the symbolic gesture, but it's an indication *for me* of how much I like a date.

This particular recipe is special to me for yet another reason: it's an encapsulation of my childhood. Reminiscent of jook, a Korean rice porridge, it's my Asian take on Italian risotto. As the son of Korean immigrants to the United States, I'm forever grateful to my mother for teaching me that a simple crumble of roasted seaweed snack makes everything taste better—and even more so when you finish a dish with sesame oil. This final imperative ingredient gives you the lip-smacking nuttiness that just brings all the flavors of the dish together.

1. In a medium pot, bring the broth to a boil, then reduce the heat to low and maintain a gentle simmer.

2. Meanwhile, in a large, deep pan over medium heat, melt the butter. Add the shallots and sauté until translucent, about 3 minutes. Add the rice and toast for 2 minutes, until it is just starting to turn golden. Add the sake and celery seeds, if using, stirring vigorously, and cook until all the liquid has evaporated.

3. Add a ladleful (about ½ cup) of the simmering broth, stirring constantly until absorbed by the rice. Repeat with the rest of the broth, one or two ladlefuls at a time, until the rice is tender, 25 to 30 minutes total.

4. Stir in the roasted seaweed, peas, sesame oil, and salt. Remove from the heat, season with more salt to taste, and serve immediately.

Chickpea Fritters

with Cilantro Mint Chutney

ANTONI POROWSKI

SERVES 4

Cilantro Mint Chutney

½ cup roasted peanuts

1 bunch fresh cilantro leaves (about 1½ cups)

1 cup fresh mint leaves

Juice of 2 limes

1 serrano chile, seeded (optional)

2 teaspoons grated fresh ginger

½ teaspoon kosher salt, plus more to taste

Chickpea Fritters

1 (15-ounce) can chickpeas, drained and rinsed

1 small zucchini, grated and squeezed of excess moisture

½ cup frozen corn, thawed

½ cup grated carrots

3 garlic cloves, grated

½ teaspoon grated fresh ginger

¼ teaspoon cayenne

½ teaspoon ground cumin

½ teaspoon ground coriander

½ teaspoon kosher salt

¼ cup chickpea flour or rice flour

2 tablespoons coconut or vegetable oil, plus more as needed

Thinly sliced mango

Growing up, I longed for structure, unconditional love, and a sense of security. While my parents did their best, I was often left to figure things out on my own, so I sought guidance from the people I looked up to. One Mother's Day, my best friend's mom taught me how to make cilantro mint chutney. I had a large container left over, so I looked through my fridge and found the ingredients to make these chickpea fritters. I took that chutney and figured out how to utilize it alongside ingredients I had at my disposal. It's a great symbol for how I've navigated through life: learn from the greats, then figure out how to make it your own. When I think about what it means to be part of the LGBTQ+ community, I relate strongly to the fact that many of us have to cut our own paths through life without a recipe to follow (no pun intended). We take what we've been given and evolve and adapt. There's a lovely freedom to that kind of life, which makes me proud to be part of the community.

1. Make the chutney: Add the peanuts to a food processor or blender and pulse until finely chopped and sand-like in texture. Add the cilantro, mint, lime juice, chile, ginger, and salt. Process until smooth. Add water, 1 tablespoon at a time, to thin the chutney to your desired texture. Taste and season with additional salt, if necessary. Refrigerate until ready to serve.

2. Make the fritters: Add the chickpeas to a large bowl and mash with a fork or the back of a spoon. Add the zucchini, corn, carrots, garlic, ginger, cayenne, cumin, coriander, salt, and chickpea flour and stir until well combined.

3. Heat 2 tablespoons of oil in a large pan over medium-high heat until nearly smoking. Scoop about 2 tablespoons of batter at a time into your palms and shape into a patty. Working in batches, place the patties in the hot oil, spacing about 2 inches apart. Fry, flipping once, until golden brown, 2 to 3 minutes per side. Transfer to a paper towel–lined plate to drain and repeat with the remaining batter, adding more oil if needed.

4. Serve the fritters warm with the chutney and some sliced mango alongside.

Bangers and Mash

DIANA YEN

SERVES 4

Onion Gravy

6 tablespoons (¾ stick) unsalted butter

2 medium yellow onions, thinly sliced

2 tablespoons all-purpose flour

1 cup dry red wine, such as Merlot

4 cups vegetable broth

1 tablespoon Dijon mustard

2 teaspoons Worcestershire sauce

Kosher salt and freshly ground black pepper

Mash

2 pounds russet potatoes, peeled and cubed

4 tablespoons (½ stick) unsalted butter, room temperature

2 tablespoons milk

Kosher salt and freshly ground pepper

I was in the honeymoon phase with my first ever (and still) girlfriend when I came up with this dish. As a cook and a recipe writer, one of the most intimate, personal things I can do for loved ones is create recipes just for them. My girlfriend had told me about a dish her grandma would make for her after school when she was growing up in England—classic bangers and mash with loads of onion gravy. The way she reminisced about the dish made me think it was more than just the food: it was pure nourishment from someone who cared for her, a dish that gave her comfort and joy. She went away for a few weeks on a business trip, and when she came home I surprised her with lit candles and my vegetarian interpretation of her childhood favorite, replacing the traditional sausages with a homemade lentil-based version. She told me that it was the first time in her life that someone had cooked something just for her. It was my way of quietly showing her that she is family, and I will take care of her.

1. Make the onion gravy: Melt the butter in a large heavy-bottomed pan over medium heat. Add the onions and cook until softened, about 10 minutes. Reduce the heat to medium-low. Cover and cook until the onions are caramelized, stirring occasionally, 20 to 25 minutes. Stir in the flour and cook for 2 minutes more, until light golden brown. Pour in the wine, vegetable broth, mustard, and Worcestershire sauce and stir to scrape up any browned bits from the bottom of the pan. Simmer until the gravy thickens, about 30 minutes. Season to taste with salt and pepper. Cover to keep warm until ready to serve.

2. While the gravy is simmering, prepare the lentils for the bangers: In a large saucepan, cover the lentils with cold water by 2 inches and bring to a boil over high heat. Once boiling, reduce the heat to medium and simmer until the lentils are very tender, 25 to 30 minutes. Drain well.

3. Meanwhile, make the mash: Add the potatoes to a large saucepan. Cover with cold water, then bring to a boil over medium heat and cook until the potatoes are tender, 10 to 15 minutes. Drain and allow to steam dry for 1 minute. Mix in the butter, milk, and salt and pepper to taste. Mash until fluffy and smooth. Cover to keep warm until ready to serve.

4. Make the bangers: In a medium skillet, heat the olive oil over medium-high heat. Add the onion and cook, stirring frequently, until golden, about 6 minutes. Add the garlic and cook until softened, about 2 minutes. Stir in the cumin and cayenne, then remove the pan from the heat.

5. Line a baking sheet with foil and grease generously with olive oil.

Bangers

1½ cups dried brown lentils

2 tablespoons extra-virgin olive oil, plus more for greasing

1 medium yellow onion, finely chopped

2 garlic cloves, minced

1½ teaspoons ground cumin

¼ teaspoon cayenne

¾ cup plain breadcrumbs

2 tablespoons chopped fresh parsley, plus more for garnish

1 tablespoon fresh thyme leaves

2 large eggs, lightly beaten

1 tablespoon kosher salt

½ teaspoon freshly ground black pepper

6. In a large bowl, mash together the lentils, onion mixture, breadcrumbs, parsley, thyme, eggs, salt, and pepper. Form the mixture into sausage links about 4 inches long and 1½ inches thick; you should have about 16 sausages. Place on the prepared baking sheet and brush the tops of the sausages with more olive oil.

7. Turn the broiler to high.

8. Broil the bangers, flipping once, until golden brown, about 3 minutes per side.

9. When ready to serve, warm the mash and onion gravy, if needed. Mound a generous portion of potatoes on each plate and top with sausages and gravy. Sprinkle with parsley and serve.

Spicy Bucatini Aglio e Olio

MICHAEL MARINO & JORGE MORET

SERVES 4

Kosher salt

1 pound dried bucatini

¼ cup extra-virgin olive oil

5 garlic cloves, minced

1 anchovy fillet, minced

1 tablespoon red pepper flakes

¼ cup plain breadcrumbs

¼ cup freshly grated Pecorino Romano cheese

Jorge and I met in 2008, and after three months of seriously dating, I decided to introduce him to my parents. What better way to meet my Italian family than at Sunday dinner? Jorge was nervous, but I was sure it would work out beautifully because they were always very accepting and I knew they wanted me to meet a man whom I could grow old with. (That's about the only traditional thing about them.) I had come out at a very early age to my family—I was 16 years old—so bringing Jorge home for Sunday dinner was not intimidating for me. My mom whipped up some *spaghetti aglio e olio*: a traditional Italian dish typically prepared when you don't have many ingredients available. My parents instantly liked Jorge, and he liked them right back. It was a successful meeting of all my favorite people at the dinner table. This is our take on that recipe—made with crunchy breadcrumbs, thick bucatini, and anchovies for added savoriness.

1. Bring a large pot of generously salted water to a boil over high heat. Cook the pasta in the boiling water until just shy of al dente. Reserve about 1 cup of the cooking water, then drain.

2. While the pasta is cooking, in a large skillet, heat 2 tablespoons of olive oil over medium heat. When the oil is shimmering, add the garlic and sauté until golden, about 2 minutes. Add the anchovy, red pepper flakes, and breadcrumbs. Cook for about 3 minutes, until the breadcrumbs start to crisp. Remove the pan from the heat.

3. Add the pasta to the pan with the breadcrumbs and return to medium heat. Add the remaining 2 tablespoons oil and toss well to coat. If the pasta looks dry, add the reserved pasta water, a bit at a time, and continue cooking until the pasta is tender and the sauce is silky, about 2 minutes.

4. Serve the pasta topped with freshly grated Pecorino Romano.

General Tso's Cauliflower

ZAC YOUNG

SERVES 2 TO 4

Sauce

¼ cup soy sauce

¼ cup rice wine vinegar

¼ cup mirin (sweet rice wine) or sherry

¼ cup light brown sugar

1 teaspoon toasted sesame oil

1 tablespoon cornstarch

1 tablespoon peanut or vegetable oil

3 garlic cloves, minced

1 tablespoon minced fresh ginger

6 dried red chiles or red pepper flakes to taste

Cauliflower

6 to 8 cups peanut or vegetable oil

½ cup all-purpose flour

½ cup plus 1 tablespoon cornstarch

½ teaspoon baking powder

Pinch of kosher salt

2 large egg whites

1 tablespoon vodka

1 teaspoon soy sauce

1 medium or large head of cauliflower, broken into small florets

Growing up in an almost unnervingly progressive and accepting home meant that coming out as a gay was, well, underwhelming. My "yep, I'm gay" moment unfurled in our barely used kitchen over a weekend treat of Chinese takeout. That night, my vegan mother was picking at her steamed tofu and brown rice and she asked, "Do you remember Lisa?" Of course I remembered Lisa. She had directed me in shows starting when I was just 7 years old. "She's leaving Children's Theatre of Maine and is interested in developing theater for gay and lesbian kids." As a professional therapist, my mother sure knew how to bait a hook—and that night I called her out on her fishing expedition: "If you are going to ask if I'm gay, the answer is yes. Now, can you pass the chopsticks?" Any disappointment my mother might have felt that evening was about the nutritional value of the General Tso's chicken, pan-fried pork dumplings, and quart of hot-and-sour soup I wolfed down. In memory of that night, and to make my mom proud, here's a veggie-centric version of my takeout favorite, made with cauliflower instead of chicken. Serve it with rice, noodles, or all by itself.

1. Make the sauce: In a small bowl, whisk together the soy sauce, vinegar, mirin, brown sugar, and sesame oil. Add the cornstarch and whisk to dissolve any lumps.

2. Heat the peanut oil in a large skillet over medium heat. When the oil is shimmering, add the garlic, ginger, and chiles and cook until softened, about 2 minutes. Add the soy sauce mixture and cook, stirring constantly with a rubber spatula, until boiling, about 1 minute. Remove the pan from the heat.

3. Make the cauliflower: In a large Dutch oven or heavy-bottomed pot, heat the peanut oil over medium-high heat until it reaches 350°F.

4. In a medium bowl, whisk together the flour, ½ cup cornstarch, the baking powder, and salt and set aside.

5. Add the egg whites to a large bowl and whisk briskly until lightened, about 1 minute, then add the vodka, soy sauce, and remaining tablespoon of cornstarch and whisk until incorporated.

6. Toss about half the cauliflower florets in the egg white mixture and stir to generously coat. Using one hand (which is now your "wet" hand), transfer the cauliflower a few pieces at a time to the flour mixture. Using your other hand, fully coat the cauliflower in the flour mixture, pressing lightly to adhere.

7. Carefully add about half the cauliflower at a time to the hot oil. Fry until light golden brown and the cauliflower is al dente, 3 to 5 minutes,

depending on the size of the florets. Using a slotted spoon or spider, transfer the cauliflower to a paper towel-lined plate to drain. Return the oil to 350°F before frying the remaining cauliflower.

8. Before serving, return the skillet with the sauce to medium heat and cook until warmed through. If the sauce has thickened too much, thin it by adding a bit of water, 1 tablespoon at a time, until it reaches your desired consistency. Toss the fried cauliflower in the sauce until well coated, then serve immediately.

TASTY PRIDE

Cauliflower Sandwiches

with Smoked Gouda and Peppadews

AMELIA RAMPE

SERVES 4

1 large head of cauliflower, leaves removed, trimmed

3 tablespoons extra-virgin olive oil

Kosher salt and freshly ground black pepper

1 cup shredded smoked Gouda or Provolone cheese

1 medium shallot, thinly sliced into rings

1 large garlic clove, thinly sliced

Pinch of red pepper flakes

1 bunch rainbow chard, stemmed, torn into 2-inch pieces

4 hoagie rolls

Mayonnaise

⅓ cup chopped Peppadew peppers

I was a bit of a late bloomer in terms of coming out, and after countless arguments with family members on the subject, I knew that coming out to them would not change their perspective. Finally, after marrying my husband, I knew I had the love and support I needed to speak my truth, and I came out to him. About six years later, my daughter, Anastasia, then seventeen years old, came out to me as bisexual. Thoughts raced through my mind as she started to explain herself. I thought about the various stories of people coming out to their parents—some awkward, and many painful. How I reacted in this moment could, would, shape her future and our relationship forever. I looked her in the eye, gave her a tight squeeze, and said, "Me too." A look of relief washed over her face. Nothing had changed, and just like every other night, I cooked her dinner and we sat down to eat. The meal? Cauliflower sandwiches—a favorite of ours—made with rainbow chard, Peppadew peppers, and melted Gouda cheese. Quick, flavorful, and comforting.

1. Preheat the oven to 450°F.

2. Chop the cauliflower into florets. Spread the florets in an even layer on a baking sheet. Toss them with 2 tablespoons olive oil and generously season with salt and pepper.

3. Roast the cauliflower for 20 minutes, until browned on the bottom. Gently toss the florets, then return to the oven for 5 to 10 minutes more, until golden brown and tender. Remove from the oven and divide the cauliflower into 4 piles. Immediately top each pile with the shredded cheese so it begins to melt over the cauliflower. Leave the oven on.

4. Meanwhile, heat the remaining 1 tablespoon olive oil in a large skillet over medium heat. When the oil is shimmering, add the shallot, garlic, red pepper flakes, and a pinch of salt and pepper. Cook until the shallot is tender and translucent, 2 to 3 minutes. Increase the heat to medium-high, add the chard leaves, and cook until just wilted, about 3 minutes.

5. Slice the hoagies lengthwise almost all the way through, keeping one long side intact. Place in the oven, directly on the racks, to toast, 2 to 3 minutes.

6. To assemble the sandwiches, spread mayonnaise on both sides of the toasted rolls. Carefully transfer a cauliflower pile to the bottom half of each roll, then top with the sautéed chard and Peppadew peppers. Close the rolls and serve.

Pasta Puttanesca

KAREN AKUNOWICZ

SERVES 4

Kosher salt

¼ cup high-quality olive oil

4 large garlic cloves, thinly sliced

1 (28-ounce) can crushed tomatoes, preferably San Marzano

½ cup zesty olives, such as Lucques, Cerignola, or Picholine, halved and pitted

3 anchovy fillets, chopped

1½ tablespoons capers, drained and rinsed

1 tablespoon fresh oregano leaves

½ teaspoon crushed Calabrian red pepper flakes

Freshly ground black pepper

1 pound dried linguine

2 tablespoons chopped fresh flat-leaf parsley

It all started with puttanesca. I was working at a nonprofit, just a few years out of college, and had a serious crush on a coworker—but in my not-so-subtle flirting, none of my lines were working. Then I told her I would cook for her. Her eyes lit up. "Okay, what time?" I paused. "Eight?" I gave her my address and instructed her to bring the wine. After work, I ran to my favorite bookstore, scouring the shelves for something that would transform me into a culinary goddess. I came across a recipe for puttanesca. Italian legend has it that ladies of the night would make the savory sauce to draw men into their homes. It was exactly what I needed. As I cooked it, I thought I was creating magic, watching the olive oil shimmer, the garlic sauté, and the flavors meld together into one vibrant, spicy sauce. That was the moment I fell in love with cooking: the process, the act of feeding someone, and the chemistry of it all. Looking back, I *know* that sauce was terrible. I'm sure I didn't rinse the capers, I used fresh tomatoes instead of canned, and I undoubtedly overcooked the pasta. I did, however, get the girl. Puttanesca is still one of my favorite sauces. It's quick, easy, and vibrant, with earthy piquant flavors—a perfect example of Southern Italian cooking.

1. Bring a large pot of generously salted water to a boil over high heat.

2. Meanwhile, heat the olive oil in a medium heavy-bottomed pot over medium-high heat. Add the garlic and sauté until fragrant and golden, about 30 seconds. Add the tomatoes and stir with a wooden spoon to incorporate the oil, then add the olives, anchovies, capers, oregano, and red pepper flakes. Reduce the heat to medium-low and simmer the sauce until thickened, about 8 minutes. Season with salt and pepper.

3. When the sauce is simmering, add the dried linguine to the boiling water and cook for 6 minutes at a rolling boil. Ladle about ½ cup of the pasta water into the tomato sauce, then drain the pasta.

4. Add the linguine to the sauce and continuously stir over low heat until they are well combined. Serve garnished with the parsley.

Grain Bowl

with Fried Garlic and Turmeric-Poached Egg

SANA JAVERI KADRI

SERVES 2

6 cups vegetable broth

Kosher salt or dashi stock powder

1½ cups medium-grain rice, such as brown rice or sushi rice (see Note)

1 tablespoon distilled white vinegar

1 teaspoon ground turmeric

2 large eggs

½ cup olive oil

6 garlic cloves, thinly sliced

1 cup pea shoots or other tender greens

½ cup chopped kimchi

Note: If you prefer your rice to be on the stickier side, skip the rinsing. Otherwise, rinse until the water runs clear for more distinct grains.

My coming out coincided with having to learn how to feed myself when I reached my early 20s, so food will always feel like a bit of a triumph to me. In learning how to cook, I learned how to survive and food became my life's biggest passion. By leaving Mumbai—a place that once rejected me—and eventually coming back and making peace with the place, I found myself, my queer identity, and my life's purpose, which enabled me to come home in more ways than one. Now I live between Mumbai and Oakland, the latter where I have a home with my partner, Rosie. She is my self-proclaimed carbie-Barbie, dancing-in-the-kitchen, absolute blessing of a girlfriend who has taught me to love carbs again, to eat well, and to know that my body is at its best when it's nourished. I could not love her more for it. Our kitchen is a combination of Indian, Californian, Japanese, and Northern Italian influences and everyone is always well-fed and truly full, which in itself is a joy I didn't grow up thinking I deserved. This brothy, fully loaded rice recipe is simple, but it's my ideal dinner at home. A tasty bowl of grains with my babe: the queer life I never knew was possible, and yet here we are.

1. In a medium pot over medium-high heat, combine the vegetable broth and 1 teaspoon salt. Bring to a boil, then add the rice, cover, reduce the heat to low, and simmer for about 20 minutes, or until about two-thirds of the liquid has evaporated. The rice will look moist, and there will still be bubbling broth in the pot. Remove from the heat and let rest, lid on, for at least 15 minutes or until ready to use. The rice will continue to thicken. Season to taste with more salt.

2. Fill a medium saucepan with 4 cups of water and bring to a boil over high heat. Add the vinegar and turmeric. Reduce the heat to medium-low and bring the water to a gentle simmer. Crack each egg into its own ramekin or small bowl. Using a wooden spoon, stir the water in a clockwise motion to create a whirlpool, then gently slide the eggs into the center, one at a time. Let the eggs cook for 3 to 4 minutes, until the whites are set and the yolks are still a bit runny. Use a slotted spoon to transfer the eggs to a plate lined with paper towels.

3. Heat the olive oil in a small skillet over medium heat. When the oil is shimmering, add the garlic and fry until golden brown and crisp, 2 to 3 minutes. Using a slotted spoon, transfer the fried garlic to a paper towel–lined plate and sprinkle with salt. (Reserve the infused oil for another use.)

4. To assemble, divide the rice between two serving bowls. Top each bowl with a poached egg, a handful of pea shoots, some kimchi, and some of the fried garlic. Serve warm.

Carrot Salad
with Maple Tahini Dressing

SEAN DOOLEY

SERVES 4

¼ cup tahini

2 tablespoons fresh lemon juice

1 tablespoon maple syrup

1 tablespoon toasted sesame oil

1 teaspoon kosher salt

½ teaspoon red pepper flakes

1 pound rainbow carrots

6 Medjool dates, pitted and sliced

2 tablespoons black and white sesame seeds, toasted

¼ cup fresh cilantro leaves

As a junior in college during the "don't ask, don't tell" era in New York, I struggled to find my identity in a city that seemed just as confused as I was. I took a break from my studies and committed to a year-long apprenticeship on one of the only organic farms in the region, in Jamesport on the North Fork of Long Island. Removing myself from the bustle of the city enabled me to focus on self-awareness and come to terms with my sexuality. It also allowed me the opportunity to meet other queer farmers and to gain a vast knowledge of the diversity of ingredients available but not commonly grown. One of my first tasks as an apprentice was to harvest the initial crop of spring carrots. As I had only experienced grocery store carrots previously, this was my first honest interaction with and true appreciation for such a humbling ingredient. In this recipe, I wanted to highlight the carrots raw, to preserve their color, texture, and sweetness. The salty and subtly sweet tahini dressing rounds out their earthy flavor while the cilantro lends a bright, herbal note.

1. In a liquid measuring cup or small bowl, whisk together the tahini, lemon juice, maple syrup, sesame oil, salt, and red pepper flakes. If needed, thin with water to your desired consistency.

2. Shave the carrots lengthwise with a mandolin or vegetable peeler. Place the carrot ribbons in an ice bath to retain their color and texture until ready to assemble, then drain and pat dry.

3. In a large bowl, combine the carrot ribbons and dates. Pour the dressing over and toss to coat. Transfer the salad to a serving platter and top with the sesame seeds and cilantro.

TASTY PRIDE

Parsley Salad
with Smashed Egg Vinaigrette

REBEKAH PEPPLER

SERVES 4

1 large shallot, finely chopped

1 small garlic clove, grated

2 tablespoons white wine vinegar

½ teaspoon maple syrup

1½ teaspoons whole-grain Dijon mustard

2 tablespoons fresh grapefruit juice

Fine sea salt and freshly ground black pepper

1 large egg

3 to 4 tablespoons extra-virgin olive oil

2 large bunches fresh flat-leaf parsley or other soft greens, washed, leaves only

Flaky sea salt

My ex makes a damn fine vinaigrette. Sure, punchier dressings get the bulk of attention: your Caesar, your green goddess, or—oh, *mon dieu*—your French. But there's a subtle, sexy art to an excellent vinaigrette. It doesn't conform to exact measurements or ingredients; it takes time to perfect. It demands you taste as you go, adding what's in the fridge, adjusting for salt, offering a fingertip up to taste before tweaking. When, at last, you've created something truly special from ordinary pantry items, it transforms standard leafy greens into something worth making space for on the plate. When we broke up, she took her vinaigrette-making fingertips with her and—while I'm no stranger to the kitchen—it took me time to readjust back to my single, oil-based dressing-making self. Around the same time I started to date again, I landed on this: a vinaigrette that veers into punchy-dressing territory. It's composed of those same pantry essentials, made racier with a yolky smash of four-minute egg. It's savory and sweet and tart and lightly silky—third date material, I'd say. This recipe tosses the dressing with parsley, but use whatever green things you're currently crushing on.

1. In a medium bowl, combine the shallot, garlic, vinegar, maple syrup, mustard, and grapefruit juice. Season with fine sea salt and pepper, and set aside to let the flavors meld while you make the egg.

2. Bring a small pot of water to a boil over medium-high heat. Prepare an ice bath in a small bowl. Using a slotted spoon, carefully lower the egg into the water. Cook for 4 minutes, adjusting the heat to maintain a gentle boil. Transfer the egg to the ice bath and let cool until just slightly warm, about 2 minutes.

3. Use the back of a spoon to gently crack the egg all over, then peel. Add to the shallot mixture and use a fork to smash everything together. Slowly add the olive oil, stirring with a fork to emulsify. Season with fine sea salt and pepper.

4. Put the parsley in a large serving bowl and pour the dressing over. Toss to coat, season with the flaky salt, and serve.

Beet Borscht

LIZ ALPERN

SERVES 8

4 medium tomatoes

3 tablespoons olive oil, butter, or schmaltz (rendered chicken fat)

2 medium yellow onions, sliced

2 medium carrots, chopped

4 celery stalks, chopped

1½ pounds red beets, peeled and chopped (about 3¾ cups)

8 cups chicken, vegetable, or beef broth

3 garlic cloves, smashed

2 dried bay leaves

2 tablespoons whole black peppercorns

2 tablespoons caraway seeds

2 tablespoons apple cider vinegar

Kosher salt

Sour cream, minced fresh chives, and chopped fresh dill

Note: Prepare this borscht a day ahead if possible, since this soup, like most others, will taste even better the next day.

My parents never liked beets, so despite my Eastern European roots, I grew up virtually beet-less and borscht-less. As I leaned into my culinary career and tasted many an upscale beet dish, however, everything changed. Beets impressed me with their versatility, their undeniably earthy flavor, and their dramatic color. And so when launching my Eastern European Jewish food venture, The Gefilteria, a beet borscht was among the first dishes I studied with the elders of Brighton Beach, Brooklyn. Years later, borscht was one of the first soups I cooked up for Queer Soup Night, my justice-oriented fundraising party highlighting queer chefs that featured soup at its center. And so, miraculously, despite my having grown up in a home without borscht, few dishes have come to signify home for me the way borscht has. The nourishing aroma lulls me into imaginary childhood memories while simultaneously invigorating my palate. This recipe will guide you to a basic borscht, with the added layer of an aromatic caraway-infused broth. Note that beet borscht is only one type of borscht. Green borscht and white borscht don't use beets at all! I encourage you to check those out, as well.

1. Bring a small pot of water to a boil. Prepare an ice bath in a medium bowl.

2. Score the bottoms of the tomatoes with an X, then add to the boiling water and cook for about 60 seconds, until the skins start to curl. Transfer the tomatoes to the ice bath. Once cool enough to handle, peel and chop the tomatoes, discarding the skins and seeds.

3. In a large pot, heat the olive oil over medium heat. When the oil is shimmering, add the onions and cook until golden brown, about 10 minutes. Add the carrots, celery, and beets and continue to cook until the vegetables have softened, another 10 minutes. Stir in the tomatoes and broth, using a wooden spoon to scrape up any bits stuck to the bottom of the pan. Bring to a boil.

4. While the soup is coming to a boil, gather the garlic, bay leaves, black peppercorns, and caraway seeds in a square of cheesecloth and tie into a bundle with kitchen twine.

5. Drop the cheesecloth bundle into the soup, then reduce the heat to low. Cover and simmer for about 1 hour, until the vegetables are fork-tender.

6. Remove the pot from the heat. Remove and discard the spice bundle. Purée the soup with an immersion blender to your desired consistency. Add the vinegar, 1 tablespoon at a time, and stir to combine. Season to taste with salt.

7. Ladle the soup into bowls. Serve with a generous dollop of sour cream and a sprinkling of chives and dill.

TASTY PRIDE

Asparagus Nests

with Green Garlic Salsa Verde and Soft Eggs

PREETI MISTRY

SERVES 4

3 green garlic stalks or scallions, white and green parts minced

1 cup white wine vinegar

½ cup neutral oil of choice, such as canola

1 teaspoon freshly ground black pepper

1 teaspoon kosher salt, plus more to taste

4 duck eggs or large chicken eggs

1 bunch of asparagus, trimmed

2 tablespoons unsalted butter

½ cup fresh curry leaves (see Note)

1 teaspoon minced fresh ginger

1 teaspoon Kashmiri red chile powder

2 sprigs of fresh mint, leaves finely chopped

Note: Curry leaves can be found fresh or frozen at Indian grocery stores or in a well-stocked supermarket. If you can't find them, substitute fresh basil leaves (preferably Thai basil) and a squeeze of fresh lime juice— add to the asparagus at the last minute of cooking.

Raised in an Indian immigrant household, I never tried or even knew what asparagus was until I was an adult. My wife, on the other hand, grew up eating it—and it is one of her absolute favorite vegetables. This dish really highlights the simple beauty of the highly seasonal vegetable, available locally in Oakland, California, only from April until early June, adding a burst of Indian flavor to the mix. Butter and eggs are a traditional European pairing with asparagus, and the richness of these ingredients cuts the intense bright spice notes. To me, this dish is a product of our relationship: her love of this European vegetable combined with my Indian spice.

1. In a medium bowl, whisk together the green garlic, vinegar, oil, pepper, and salt. Set aside until ready to serve.

2. Bring a large saucepan of water to a boil over medium-high heat. Prepare an ice bath in a medium bowl.

3. Gently lower the eggs into the boiling water and cook for 6 minutes. Transfer the eggs to the ice bath with a slotted spoon. Let cool for about 5 minutes, then peel.

4. Chop the asparagus into 2-inch pieces.

5. Heat the butter in a medium pan over medium heat until it starts to brown, about 2 minutes. Add the curry leaves and ginger, and sweat them for about 1 minute, until fragrant. The curry leaves may crackle and pop slightly.

6. Add the asparagus and cook until it is tender but still has some bite, 5 to 7 minutes, depending on thickness. Season with the chile powder and salt. Remove the pan from the heat.

7. Arrange the asparagus in circles on each of the four serving plates to create "nests." Place a soft cooked egg in the center of each nest. Drizzle with the salsa verde and garnish with the mint. Serve immediately.

Serve Alongside

Hoppin' John Salad
with Warm Duck Fat Vinaigrette

LORRAINE LANE & DEBORAH VANTRECE

SERVES 12

Salad

4 (15-ounce) cans black-eyed peas, drained and rinsed

1½ cups cooked white rice, cooled

1 cup crumbled cooked bacon

2 red bell peppers, cored, seeded, and diced

1 medium red onion, diced

4 medium tomatoes, diced

2 celery stalks, diced

½ cup thinly sliced scallion greens

¼ cup chopped fresh flat-leaf parsley

2 jalapeños, seeded (optional) and minced

2 tablespoons balsamic vinegar

1 teaspoon kosher salt

1 teaspoon black pepper

3 cups stemmed and sliced kale

Dressing

½ cup duck fat or high-quality olive oil

2 garlic cloves, smashed

3 tablespoons minced shallots

½ cup apple cider vinegar

2 tablespoons Dijon mustard

3 tablespoons honey

1 teaspoon seasoning salt, such as Lawry's

1 teaspoon onion powder

1 teaspoon garlic powder

Talk about an unlikely combination—black-eyed peas and duck fat salad—but it's a true Lorraine and Deborah collaboration. That's what happens when a city girl meets a country girl, when a diva with long legs, sophistication, and style is paired with the simplicity of Peppermint Patty. Our love of food and cooking has been an important part of our relationship, from the day we met to the opening of our restaurant, Twisted Soul Cookhouse & Pours, and beyond. Lorraine is the talent and Deborah—well, in this recipe—is the peas. We found partnership in the kitchen early on by combining Southern country favorites with culinary flair. We love to add a twist to basic Southern ingredients. In this recipe, the underused legume takes on an amazing flavor when paired with the richness of duck fat—but you can use a high-quality olive oil if your grocery store or butcher does not carry duck fat. Our partnership in marriage and business is represented in our cooking style, and this recipe is the perfect example.

1. Make the salad: In a large bowl, combine the black-eyed peas, rice, bacon, bell peppers, onion, tomatoes, celery, scallion, parsley, jalapeños, balsamic vinegar, salt, and pepper. Toss well.

2. Make the dressing: Melt the duck fat in a medium skillet over medium heat. Add the garlic and shallots and cook about 5 minutes, until softened. Remove the pan from the heat.

3. In a food processor, combine the vinegar, mustard, honey, seasoning salt, onion powder, and garlic powder. Process until well combined. Slowly drizzle in the duck fat mixture and process to incorporate.

4. Pour the warm vinaigrette over the salad and toss gently to coat. Add the kale and toss again, then serve immediately.

Ciabatta Stuffing
with Leeks and Mushrooms

LUKAS VOLGER

SERVES 6 TO 8

1 (1-pound) ciabatta loaf, torn into 1½-inch pieces (about 12 cups)

6 tablespoons (¾ stick) unsalted butter, plus more for greasing

2 cups vegetable broth

1 heaping tablespoon white miso

3 leeks, white and pale green parts only, cleaned and thinly sliced

Kosher salt

10 ounces cremini mushrooms, stemmed and quartered

4 ounces shiitake mushrooms, stemmed and quartered

3 tablespoons chopped fresh parsley

3 tablespoons minced fresh chives

Freshly ground black pepper

In the summer of 2007, I moved in with my first boyfriend—and I was already plotting to host our first Thanksgiving. As November neared, I began working on the menu, but in execution, I only got as far as the shopping list. That's because less than a week before the holiday, he casually crushed my dream by admitting he would rather go to the dinner his friends were hosting. "Why don't you just cook something to bring?" he suggested as a consolation prize, which is what I did: a cornbread stuffing that turned me off the dish forever. We broke up a few months later. But I started to learn something about holiday cooking, which is that compromise and collaboration are essential ingredients. I relinquished my Thanksgiving fantasy of complete control and fantasized, instead, about the day I'd jointly host one with a partner, gathering our family of friends over everyone's own expressions of holiday food. And I excised from my repertoire cornbread stuffing, which is too crumbly, too sweet, and will always have a sour taste to me. This dish, instead, has become my go-to. Underneath its golden crunchy top it is soft and savory, packed with tender leeks and juicy mushrooms, and it doesn't skimp on the butter. It's so delicious you can serve it during any season and for any occasion.

1. Preheat the oven to 300°F. Spread the torn bread in a layer on a baking sheet. Bake for 15 minutes, until dried out. Transfer to a large bowl.

2. Increase the oven temperature to 400°F. Grease a 12-inch round cast-iron skillet or a 9 by 13-inch baking dish with butter. In a large liquid measuring cup, whisk together the vegetable broth and miso paste.

3. Melt 3 tablespoons butter in a large wide pan over medium heat. Add the leeks and season with salt. Cook, stirring occasionally, until softened and sweet, 10 to 12 minutes, reducing the heat level if the leeks begin to burn. Transfer to the bowl with the bread.

4. Return the pan to the heat. Melt the remaining 3 tablespoons butter, then add the mushrooms. Cook, stirring very occasionally, until tender and caramelized, about 8 minutes. Season with salt. Increase the heat to medium-high and pour in a splash of the broth mixture. Use a wooden spoon to scrape up all the browned bits from the bottom of the skillet. Add the mushrooms and any liquid in the pan to the bowl with the bread and leeks, along with the parsley and chives.

5. Pour the remaining broth into the bowl, folding with a spatula until the bread absorbs the liquid. Season with pepper. Transfer the mixture to the prepared skillet, pressing down with a spatula to smooth the surface and spread evenly, then cover with foil. Bake for 20 minutes, then remove the foil and bake for 20 to 30 minutes more, until lightly browned and crisp on the top and somewhat set. Serve warm directly from the pan.

TASTY PRIDE

Roasted Summer Vegetable Couscous

JAKE COHEN

SERVES 6 TO 8

1 medium zucchini, cut into ½-inch pieces

1 medium summer squash, cut into ½-inch pieces

1 red bell pepper, cored, seeded, and cut into ½-inch pieces

1 yellow bell pepper, cored, seeded, and cut into ½-inch pieces

6 tablespoons olive oil

½ teaspoon Aleppo pepper flakes or red pepper flakes

2 teaspoons kosher salt, plus more to taste

2 cups cherry tomatoes, halved

2 cups pearled couscous

4 ounces feta cheese, crumbled

½ cup minced fresh flat-leaf parsley

½ cup minced fresh dill

2 tablespoons minced fresh tarragon

Zest and juice of 1 lemon

There's a rainbow of vegetables in this recipe, but that's just scratching the surface of how queer this couscous actually is. You see, my husband and I never had many gay friends, and as we sought to find our community, we were simultaneously figuring out what role Judaism would play in our lives. We decided that hosting a queer Shabbat was the answer to both dilemmas, and would serve as a way to gather community while connecting to an age-old Jewish tradition. We brought together colleagues, acquaintances, and friends in my mother's apartment, where, alongside a feast of torn challah, a lush cheese board, and a platter of za'atar-crusted salmon, stood an overflowing bowl of Israeli couscous. It was a magical evening during which queer Jews gathered together to break bread. This recipe is my summer version, incorporating roasted squash, bell peppers, and cherry tomatoes, paired with feta and an herby dressing. The best part? You can swap any of the herbs, spices, and veggies to fit your preference and season. Add the protein of your choosing and you've got yourself a complete meal. I never expected my pride as a Jew would intertwine with my pride as a gay man, but here we are with a technicolor bowl of couscous—a recipe of which I'm naturally very proud.

1. Preheat the oven to 450°F.

2. In a large bowl, toss the zucchini, summer squash, and bell peppers with 2 tablespoons of olive oil, the Aleppo pepper, and 1 teaspoon salt. Transfer to a baking sheet and roast until tender, about 15 minutes.

3. Turn on the broiler. Add the cherry tomatoes to the pan of roasted vegetables and toss to combine. Broil until the tomatoes are golden and slightly blistered, about 4 minutes.

4. Meanwhile, in a small saucepan, bring 2¾ cups of water to a boil. Season with 1 teaspoon of salt and stir in the couscous. Reduce the heat to low, cover, and simmer until the water is almost completely absorbed and the couscous is tender, 8 to 10 minutes. Remove the pan from the heat and let sit uncovered for 10 minutes, until the remaining water is fully absorbed, then fluff with a fork.

5. Transfer the roasted vegetables and couscous to a large bowl and toss with the remaining 4 tablespoons olive oil, the feta, parsley, dill, tarragon, and lemon zest and juice. Season with more salt to taste, then serve warm or at room temperature.

Pan-Seared Artichokes
with an Aioli Trio

ADAM MERRIN & RYAN ALVAREZ

SERVES 4

Artichokes

2 large artichokes

4 large garlic cloves, minced

4 teaspoons olive oil

Flaky sea salt

4 teaspoons fresh lemon juice

Lemon Garlic Aioli

6 tablespoons mayonnaise

Zest of 1 lemon

1 tablespoon fresh lemon juice

1 large garlic clove, grated

¼ teaspoon freshly ground black pepper

⅛ teaspoon kosher salt

Spicy Harissa Aioli

¼ cup mayonnaise

2 to 3 teaspoons harissa paste, or to taste

1 large garlic clove, grated

¼ teaspoon smoked paprika

⅛ teaspoon kosher salt

We've been together for eighteen years. Our first kiss was on September 23, 2001, in Adam's tiny bachelor pad while we watched the Ken Burns documentary *Jazz*, and we've been together ever since. When we first started dating, our cooking repertoire was somewhat limited; a home-cooked candlelit dinner would involve pasta and store-bought marinara sauce straight from the jar. While our skills in the kitchen have progressed over the years, our love for sharing a quiet, romantic meal at home hasn't changed. Artichokes are said to be an aphrodisiac, so this hearty appetizer is perfect for a date night in. In this simple recipe, halved artichokes are filled with minced garlic and a drizzle of olive oil, then baked in the oven until steaming hot. For extra flavor, the artichokes are grilled until charred and smoky, then brightened with a squeeze of lemon. With three tasty aioli sauces for your dipping pleasure—tangy dill, lemon garlic, and spicy harissa—this is an easy recipe that we could have pulled off even back in 2001.

1. Preheat the oven to 425°F.

2. Wash the artichokes, then trim the stems to 2 inches in length. If any sharp spines remain on the tips of the leaves, snip them off with kitchen shears. Using a sharp serrated knife, cut 2 inches off the tops of the artichokes, making them flat. Place the artichokes flat side down and cut in half vertically, from the stem to the leaves. Using a sturdy metal spoon, scoop out the fuzzy "choke" in the center and discard.

3. Place one of the artichoke halves on a square of foil, cut side up. Take one clove of minced garlic and press the pieces of garlic between the leaves, evenly distributing throughout. Drizzle 1 teaspoon of olive oil over the top, then sprinkle with a generous pinch of flaky sea salt. Lift the corners of the foil and wrap the artichoke snugly, folding the top to seal. Place on a rimmed baking sheet. Repeat with the remaining artichoke halves.

4. Bake the artichokes for about 40 minutes, or until the hearts are completely tender when pierced with a knife.

Tangy Dill Aioli

¼ cup mayonnaise

1½ teaspoons white wine
vinegar

⅛ teaspoon dried dill

⅛ teaspoon garlic powder

⅛ teaspoon smoked
paprika

⅛ teaspoon kosher salt

⅛ teaspoon freshly ground
black pepper

5. While the artichokes are roasting, make the aioli trio: For the lemon garlic aioli, mix the mayonnaise, lemon zest and juice, garlic, pepper, and salt in a small bowl.

6. For the harissa aioli, mix the mayonnaise, harissa, garlic, paprika, and salt in a separate small bowl.

7. For the dill aioli, mix the mayonnaise, vinegar, dill, garlic powder, paprika, salt, and pepper in another small bowl.

8. Preheat a grill, grill pan, or heavy skillet over medium heat.

9. When the artichokes are finished roasting, open the foil packages carefully (the steam inside will be very hot). Place the artichoke halves cut side down on the hot grill. Cook until blackened grill marks appear, 1 to 2 minutes.

10. Transfer the artichokes to a serving plate, and drizzle with the lemon juice. Serve immediately with the aioli trio.

Mississippi Corn Pudding

ELLE SIMONE SCOTT

SERVES 12

5 tablespoons unsalted butter, melted and cooled slightly, plus more for greasing

2 large eggs, beaten

⅓ cup sugar

½ cup whole milk

¼ cup heavy cream

¾ cup sour cream

½ cup all-purpose flour

½ cup coarse yellow cornmeal

1 teaspoon kosher salt

⅛ teaspoon white pepper

⅛ teaspoon paprika

⅛ teaspoon baking soda

¼ cup chopped yellow onion

½ cup chopped celery

1 pound fresh corn kernels, cut from 4 cobs

1 cup shredded cheddar cheese

1 cup butter cracker crumbs, such as Ritz

I don't remember ever hearing or using the word *accepted* in my family. I think that's because the notion of not being accepted was unheard of. Holidays were the times when we expected to see one another, no matter how near or far we were during the rest of the year. Any disagreements and misunderstandings were left outside the door. And when you come from a family of amazing cooks like I do, seeing what kind of dishes would come to the table was always exciting. My cousins and I like to re-create those dishes from our family history—dishes that taste complex and have so much depth of flavor. We've realized some of the recipes are more involved, while others are simple and tasty, like this one—my grandmother's corn pudding. It's a savory side that's great hot out of the oven, or even cold for a quick midday snack. It brings back memories of seeing my granny placing it on the table at dinnertime and my later scooping spoonfuls of it from the fridge late in the night. I hope it brings you as much joy as it has brought me all these years.

1. Set a rack in the lower third of the oven. Preheat the oven to 350°F. Grease a 9 by 13-inch casserole dish with butter, making sure to get in all the corners and sides of the dish.

2. In a medium bowl, whisk together the eggs and sugar until well combined. Add the melted butter, milk, heavy cream, and sour cream and whisk to incorporate.

3. In a large bowl, whisk together the flour, cornmeal, salt, pepper, paprika, and baking soda.

4. Using a spatula, fold the wet ingredients, 1 cup at a time, into the dry ingredients until well combined.

5. Fold in the onion, celery, corn, and cheese.

6. Pour the batter into the prepared baking dish and sprinkle the cracker crumbs on top. Bake the pudding for 30 to 40 minutes, rotating halfway through, until lightly browned on top and the tip of a knife inserted in the center comes out clean.

Coconut Creamed Kale
with Bacon (Laing)

WOLDY REYES

SERVES 4 TO 6

8 ounces thick-cut uncured bacon, chopped

1 medium shallot, minced

5 garlic cloves, minced

3 Thai chiles, thinly sliced

1 (1½-inch) piece fresh ginger, peeled and grated

1 tablespoon fish sauce

1 (13.5-ounce) can full-fat unsweetened coconut milk

Kosher salt and freshly ground black pepper

2 large bunches lacinato (Tuscan) kale, thick ribs and stems removed, leaves torn

Lime wedges

When I was growing up, one of my favorite foods was a Filipino side dish traditionally made with taro leaves stewed in creamy coconut milk, with spicy chiles, aromatic ginger, and pork; it was called *laing*, and is similar to creamed spinach. In my family, we would serve it at large gatherings as one of the countless dishes we would pile onto our plates, stuffing our faces until our pants would burst open. Now that I'm older, I'm trying to share with my boyfriend the food culture I grew up enjoying. Laing was a big part of my childhood, and when I first cooked it for him, he told me it tasted muddy. *Muddy?* I was insulted! To his American palate, the soft texture was a difficult bridge to cross. I was disappointed he didn't love it, but it inspired me to re-create and modernize my childhood favorite. I brightened the flavor by using lacinato kale instead of taro leaves, and instead of stewing the kale, I quickly coated the leaves in a rich coconut sauce. As a result, I'm happy to report my boyfriend now loves laing—and we've made a new food memory together.

1. Heat a large cast-iron skillet or Dutch oven over medium heat. Add the bacon and cook until crispy and brown, about 8 minutes. Transfer the bacon from the pan with a slotted spoon to a paper towel–lined plate to drain, leaving the rendered fat behind.

2. Add the shallot to the pan, reduce the heat to medium-low, and sauté for 2 minutes, until translucent. Add the garlic, chiles, and ginger. Continue cooking for 3 minutes more, until very fragrant and the garlic starts to brown.

3. Add the fish sauce and coconut milk and stir with a wooden spoon, scraping up any browned bits from the bottom of the pan. Bring the sauce to a simmer and cook, stirring, for 5 minutes, until thickened slightly. Season to taste with salt and pepper.

4. Remove the pan from the heat, add the kale, and toss until well coated. Season with more salt and pepper.

5. Transfer the creamed kale to a serving bowl and add a squeeze of lime juice. Top with the crispy bacon bits, then serve with more lime wedges alongside.

Rainbow Brussels Sprouts Salad

VAUGHN VREELAND

SERVES 6

2 medium shallots, sliced

2 jalapeños, seeded and sliced into half-moons (optional)

Zest and juice of 1 lemon, plus more juice to taste

1 tablespoon red wine vinegar

Kosher salt and freshly ground black pepper

1 cup pine nuts

1 pound Brussels sprouts

1 large ruby red grapefruit

½ cup pomegranate seeds

½ cup grated carrots

½ cup corn kernels, fresh or frozen and thawed

3 sprigs of fresh mint, leaves chopped, plus more for garnish

¼ cup chopped fresh cilantro, plus more for garnish

¼ cup olive oil

Shaved Pecorino Romano cheese

I grew up in North Carolina, where summertime was always centered on my mom's garden. I'd spend hours grazing among the clouds of fresh mint and tiptoeing through rows of hot peppers. Food is paramount in my family. Touchstone culinary memories like this one from childhood are what drove me to a life of food journalism. I vividly remember setting bananas Foster ablaze (supervised) and almost taking my kitchen down with it. Or making french fries in a piping-hot olive oil bath (unsupervised) and *actually* taking my kitchen down with it. Those moments in the kitchen with my family bonded us. My parents' undying support has been nothing but overwhelming—even during those rather questionable first attempts in the kitchen. My mom's willingness to let me make mistakes was essential to my growing into the confident gay man I am today. This recipe is special to me because it is inspired by my family's favorite side dish at the holidays. It's inspired by the colors and flavors of my mom's garden, only a little fresher and a little gayer.

1. In a small bowl, combine the shallots, jalapeños, if using, lemon zest and juice, and vinegar. Season with salt and pepper. Allow the shallots to lightly pickle, stirring occasionally, while you assemble the rest of the salad.

2. In a medium skillet over low heat, toast the pine nuts until golden brown and fragrant, shaking the pan frequently, 3 to 5 minutes. Transfer to a bowl and set aside until ready to assemble the salad.

3. Trim the ends from the Brussels sprouts. Using the slicing attachment on a food processor or a sharp knife, thinly shave the sprouts. Toss them in a large bowl with salt and pepper (this will ensure the salad is well seasoned throughout).

4. Supreme the grapefruit by cutting off the top and bottom so it sits flat on a cutting board. Cut away the peel and pith to fully expose the flesh. Cut the grapefruit segments from between the connective membranes, then slice each segment in half crosswise so that you're left with 1-inch pieces.

5. Add the grapefruit segments, shallots and their pickling liquid, pine nuts, pomegranate seeds, carrots, corn, mint, cilantro, and olive oil to the shaved sprouts and toss well. Season with salt, pepper, and more lemon juice, if desired. Refrigerate until ready to serve. Before serving, top the salad with shaved Pecorino and more mint and cilantro.

Corn on the Cob
with Harissa Honey Butter

JESSICA BATTILANA

SERVES 6

4 tablespoons (½ stick) unsalted butter, room temperature

2 tablespoons harissa, homemade (recipe follows) or store-bought

2 tablespoons honey

6 ears of corn, shucked

My wife and I left the East Coast for San Francisco in the spring of 2005. There were many things for us to fall in love with—including the obvious queerness of the place and the giant Pride flag that flew over the Castro neighborhood like a superhero's rainbow cape. Though we were already in our mid-twenties then, this city was the place where we became more fully realized versions of ourselves. It's also where I fell in love with Mexican-style corn on the cob. Impaled on thick wooden skewers, the ears are brushed with mayonnaise, lavished with crumbled Cotija cheese, and splashed with hot sauce. This unfamiliar riff on a familiar vegetable tasted like freedom to me. The memory of that street snack inspired this recipe. I spike the butter with homemade harissa and spread it generously over the grilled ears of corn. A drizzle of honey balances the spice, and one final turn on the grill caramelizes the kernels.

1. Preheat a charcoal or gas grill on high, or a grill pan over medium-high heat.

2. In a small bowl, stir together the butter, harissa, and honey.

3. Place the corn on the grill and cook, turning occasionally, until slightly charred and cooked through, 8 to 10 minutes if using a charcoal or gas grill, or 15 to 20 minutes if using a grill pan.

4. Transfer the corn to a plate and brush the ears liberally all over with the harissa butter, then return them to the grill and cook for 1 minute more, just until the honey caramelizes. Transfer to a platter and serve immediately.

Harissa

MAKES ¾ CUP

2 tablespoons tomato paste

1½ teaspoons cayenne, plus more to taste

1½ teaspoons smoked paprika

1 teaspoon kosher salt, plus more to taste

1 teaspoon ground cumin

¾ teaspoon ground coriander

¾ teaspoon ground caraway

2 garlic cloves

1 jarred roasted red bell pepper

¼ cup extra-virgin olive oil

Note: You can brush any extra harissa on chicken before grilling, spoon it onto store-bought hummus, or use it to dress up roasted or grilled vegetables.

In the bowl of a food processor, combine the tomato paste, cayenne, paprika, salt, cumin, coriander, caraway, garlic, red pepper, and olive oil. Process until smooth. Season to taste with more cayenne and salt. Store in an airtight container in the refrigerator for up to 1 week, or frozen for up to 3 months.

Rice Salad

with Nuts and Sour Cherries

YOTAM OTTOLENGHI

SERVES 6 TO 8

Scant 1 cup (150 grams) wild rice

Scant 1¼ cups (220 grams) basmati rice

5½ tablespoons (80 milliliters) olive oil

1¼ teaspoons kosher salt, plus more to taste

1⅓ cups (330 milliliters) boiling water

⅔ cup (100 grams) quinoa

6½ tablespoons (60 grams) almonds, skins on, coarsely chopped

7 tablespoons (60 grams) pine nuts

¼ cup (60 milliliters) sunflower oil, or other neutral oil of choice

2 medium onions, thinly sliced (about 3 cups/ 320 grams)

Freshly ground black pepper

1 cup (30 grams) fresh flat-leaf parsley leaves, coarsely chopped

⅔ cup (20 grams) fresh basil leaves, coarsely chopped

⅓ cup (10 grams) fresh tarragon leaves, coarsely chopped

2 cups (40 grams) arugula

⅔ cup (80 grams) dried sour cherries

¼ cup (60 milliliters) lemon juice

Zest of 1 lemon

2 garlic cloves, crushed

I love to cook as a way to show affection for others, and to me, a good dish has many of the same qualities as a good relationship—lots of different elements joining together to create something that is greater than the sum of its parts. In this case, a variety of textures, colors, and flavors offer a lovely bit of discovery and surprise in every bite. It's satisfying, sustaining, and, with grains, nuts, herbs, and fruit, a bit good for you and a bit indulgent at the same time. Strong qualities to seek out in both meals and in partners.

1. Place the wild rice in a saucepan, cover with plenty of water, bring to a boil, and then reduce the heat to low and gently simmer for 35 minutes, until the rice is cooked but still firm. Drain, rinse under cold water, and set aside to dry.

2. Mix the basmati rice with 1 tablespoon of the olive oil and ½ teaspoon salt. Place in a saucepan with the boiling water, cover, and cook over the lowest possible heat for 15 minutes. Remove from the heat, uncover, place a tea towel over the pan, replace the lid, and set aside for 10 minutes. Uncover and allow to cool down completely.

3. Bring a small saucepan of water to a boil and add the quinoa. Cook for 9 minutes, then drain into a fine-mesh sieve, refresh under cold water, and set aside.

4. Place the almonds and pine nuts in a small pan with 1 tablespoon of the olive oil and a pinch of salt. Cook over medium-low heat for about 5 minutes, stirring frequently. Transfer to a small plate as soon as the pine nuts begin to color and set aside.

5. Heat the sunflower oil in a large sauté pan and add the onions, ¼ teaspoon salt, and some black pepper. Cook over high heat for 5 to 8 minutes, stirring often, so that parts of the onion get crisp and others just soft. Transfer to paper towels to drain.

6. Place all the grains in a large bowl along with the chopped herbs, arugula, fried onions, nuts, and sour cherries. Add the lemon juice and zest, the remaining 3½ tablespoons olive oil, the garlic, ½ teaspoon salt, and some pepper. Mix well and set aside for at least 10 minutes before serving.

Sweets

TASTY PRIDE

Fudgy Miso Brownies

RUBY TANDOH

MAKES 24 BROWNIES

1 cup plus 6 tablespoons (2¾ sticks) unsalted butter

10 ounces dark chocolate

3 to 5 ounces (⅓ to ½ cup) white miso paste, or to taste

2 teaspoons vanilla extract

2 cups sugar

4 large eggs

1 cup all-purpose flour

1 cup unsweetened cocoa powder

I refuse to choose between salty and sweet. I like flakes of sea salt on chocolate, salted butter in pound cake, and handfuls of popcorn both savory and tooth-shatteringly sweet. I like salted potato chips shoved into my mouth while a square of milk chocolate melts on my tongue. I'm sorry, I'm gross, I know. But I will not choose. I suppose what I should really do, as a hungry bisexual, is play down the power of my fickle appetite. I should pick one or the other, or, if I must love both, I should do so with restraint. And I have tried to in the past—I really have. When I've loved men, I've tried hard to love only men. When I've loved women, I've worked overtime to prove that I am serious about it, that I won't betray the queer cause. I have swung wildly from one allegiance to another, each time losing sight of what (or whom) I really crave, each time losing my center of gravity far outside of myself. But now, I refuse to choose. I want sweet, salty, sticky, crisp, buttery, fresh, heavy, featherweight everything. I hold all these contradictions within me. I am hungry for all things at once. These brownies, with their combination of dark chocolate and savory white miso, are the perfect example of enjoying all things at once.

1. Preheat the oven to 350°F. Set a rack in the center of the oven. Line a 9 by 13-inch baking pan with parchment paper.

2. Bring a small pot of water to a gentle simmer. Set a large heatproof bowl over the pot, making sure the bottom is not touching the water, and add the butter and chocolate. Melt, stirring occasionally, until smooth and glossy, about 5 minutes. (You can also do this in the microwave: heat the mixture in 20-second intervals, stirring between.)

3. Remove the bowl from the pot and stir in the miso paste, starting small and adding more to taste. (Remember that the saltiness will be muted by the addition of the sugar, eggs, and flour.) Stir in the vanilla.

4. In a separate large bowl, beat the sugar and eggs together with a balloon whisk (or an electric hand mixer) for about 5 minutes, until the mixture is densely foamy, thick, and almost doubled in volume.

5. Spoon a third of the beaten egg and sugar mixture into the chocolate mixture, stirring briskly. Slowly add the remaining egg mixture, folding it in with a rubber spatula to keep in as much air as possible. Once the batter is almost combined (there should still be a few streaks), sift in the flour and cocoa powder and gently fold until smooth.

6. Pour the batter into the prepared pan and bake for 25 to 27 minutes, or until the brownies are barely set. They should still be soft and fudgy in the center, but no longer raw or gooey. Remove from the oven and let cool completely in the pan. They will sink a little, becoming pleasingly chewy and smooth. Once cooled, slice into 24 pieces.

Lime Soufflés
with Summer Berries

ORLANDO SOTO

SERVES 8

Melted butter, for greasing pan

⅓ cup granulated sugar, plus more for sprinkling

1 pound mixed berries, plus more for filling soufflés

Juice of 1 lime

3 large eggs, separated, plus 5 large egg whites, room temperature

1 cup whole milk

3 tablespoons cornstarch

½ cup full-fat plain yogurt

Zest of 2 limes

1¼ cups sifted confectioners' sugar

Growing up in Puerto Rico, I never imagined I'd become a pastry chef in New York City. I was an only child and the first male of my generation in the family. I went to engineering school, worked in biomedical research labs, and was well on my way to achieving the ideal "alpha role" in my family. Then, in my junior year of college, I fell in love with a man. I didn't want to fail my family, or hurt them and their dreams, so I kept it a secret. But upon graduating, I announced that I was moving to New York City to pursue a career in pastry. I broke up with my then-boyfriend because I was afraid to come out, and for the next several years I worked in kitchens and focused solely on proving I could succeed in my chosen career. But then it happened again. I fell in love and held back, not letting the relationship grow and fully mature. That summer, while in the midst of making soufflés for dinner service at Café Boulud, I realized that despite all the good work I was doing for my career, I hadn't made efforts to foster my own romantic happiness. I had to step up for myself and for my truth—and to be able to fully love another human being. Now every time I make these soufflés, I go back to that moment and I feel lighter, standing tall in love. This recipe, made with fresh berries and bright lime zest, is a delicious homage to that journey.

1. Preheat the oven to 350°F.

2. Brush butter on the bottoms and up the sides of eight 4-ounce ramekins. Sprinkle sugar in a ramekin and tilt to coat, then tap out the excess into the next ramekin and continue until all are coated.

3. In a medium bowl, toss the berries with the lime juice and a bit of sugar, depending on how sweet they are. Set aside to macerate while you prepare the soufflés.

4. In a separate medium bowl, whisk together the egg yolks, ⅓ cup sugar, and the milk until combined. Add the cornstarch and whisk until smooth. Transfer the mixture to a small pot over medium-high heat. Cook, whisking constantly, until the custard thickens, about 5 minutes. Transfer to a large bowl and spread on the bottom to cool a bit. Whisk in the yogurt and lime zest.

5. In a stand mixer fitted with the whisk attachment, whip the egg whites on medium speed until foamy and doubled in volume, about 90 seconds. With the mixer running, add half the confectioners' sugar. Increase the speed to very high, and whip until the meringue is doubled in volume, about 1 minute. Reduce the speed to medium and add the remaining confectioners' sugar. Increase the speed again to very high and whip for 30 to 45 seconds more. The meringue should be smooth and soft, but hold its shape.

6. Scoop about 1 cup of the meringue into the yogurt mixture and whisk to combine. Gently fold in the rest of the meringue, half at a time, using a wide rubber spatula to keep the meringue from deflating.

7. Transfer the soufflé batter to a zippered plastic bag. Snip off a corner to make about a dime-sized opening. Gently pipe the batter into the ramekins, filling halfway. Set the batter aside and place 2 or 3 berries at the very center of each ramekin. Cover with more batter, filling the ramekins to just above the rim, without overflowing. Gently tap the ramekins on the counter to smooth the surface. Bake for 16 to 18 minutes, until the soufflés have risen nearly 1 inch above the rims of the ramekins, are golden brown on top, and jiggle only slightly when gently shaken.

8. Serve the soufflés hot, with macerated berries alongside to spoon into the soufflé as you eat.

Malted Dark Chocolate Fudge Pie

BO DURHAM

SERVES 8

Pie Dough

2 cups all-purpose flour, plus more for dusting

2 tablespoons granulated sugar

½ teaspoon kosher salt

10 tablespoons (1¼ sticks) unsalted butter, cubed and chilled

2 large egg yolks

4 tablespoons ice water

Malted Chocolate Cream Filling

2 cups heavy cream

½ cup whole milk

1⅓ cups malted milk powder

1 tablespoon vanilla extract

1 teaspoon kosher salt

4 tablespoons granulated sugar

5 large egg yolks

6 ounces dark chocolate, chopped

4 ounces milk chocolate, chopped

Chocolate Whipped Cream

2 cups heavy cream

¼ cup sifted confectioners' sugar

2 tablespoons cocoa powder

1 tablespoon vanilla extract

1 (5-ounce) package of malted milk balls, crushed

I always knew I was different as a child; it wasn't until I grew older that I was able to accept my identity and begin living my truth. I've been an out and proud homosexual since my freshman year of high school, but I didn't start living the truest version of myself until recently, in my late 20s. I may not be sporty or a writer, but I am a *fierce* pastry chef—this much I know. And despite this fact, and despite baking for a living, I never actually attempted to make a classic cream pie until many years into my career. Cake has long been my go-to, but I've always been a fan of pies. This recipe is my take on a chocolate cream pie, made with malted milk powder for depth and rich dark chocolate. It can be garnished with chocolate sprinkles, shaved chocolate, or crushed malted milk balls. The latter are my personal favorite—I'm lucky if any of them actually make it to the finished product. Now, let them eat pie!

1. Make the pie dough: Sift the flour, sugar, and salt together into a large bowl. Using only your fingertips, pinch the cubes of butter into the flour, breaking up the butter as you go, until no large lumps remain. Shake the bowl to force the large chunks of butter to the surface.

2. Mix the egg yolks and ice water together in a small bowl with a fork until evenly combined. Add the liquid to the flour mixture, reserving 1 tablespoon or so in case you don't need all of it—you don't want the pastry to be too wet. Quickly mix everything with a fork until the dough just starts to come together. Add more liquid to the driest parts of the dough, if needed. The dough is ready when it holds together in a ball when squeezed in your palm. Transfer the dough to a clean surface and bring the dough together in a disc with no cracks or dry bits. Wrap the dough in plastic wrap and chill for at least 30 minutes, or up to 4 days.

3. Preheat the oven to 350°F.

4. Lightly flour a clean surface and unwrap the chilled dough. Flour the top of the dough. Using a rolling pin, push down on the dough, giving it a quarter turn every few smushes, to spread the dough evenly and ensure it doesn't stick to the surface. Start to roll out the dough, continuing to turn. If any cracks form, smush them back together. Roll out the dough to a circle about ⅛ inch thick. Carefully transfer to a 9½-inch pie dish. Crimp the edges as desired. Line the crust with parchment paper and fill with pie weights or dried beans.

5. Blind-bake the crust for 20 to 30 minutes. Carefully lift the parchment to remove the pie weights, then bake for another 5 to 10 minutes, until the crust is light golden brown. Remove from the oven and let cool completely.

6. Make the filling: In a medium pot, combine the cream, milk, malted milk powder, vanilla, salt, and 2 tablespoons of sugar. Bring to a gentle simmer over medium heat, whisking frequently so the mixture doesn't scald or clump.

7. In a medium bowl, whisk together the egg yolks and remaining 2 tablespoons sugar. Add about ½ cup of the warm cream mixture and whisk to combine. Pour the mixture into the pan with the remaining cream mixture and cook, stirring constantly, until the mixture is thick enough to coat the back of a spoon, about 5 minutes.

8. Add the dark and milk chocolates to a large bowl and pour in the warm custard through a fine-mesh sieve. Whisk until the chocolate is melted and the mixture is smooth. Pour the chocolate custard into the cooled crust. Refrigerate for at least 4 hours, or overnight, until the custard is set.

9. Make the chocolate whipped cream: In the bowl of a stand mixer fitted with a whisk attachment, combine the cream, confectioners' sugar, cocoa powder, and vanilla. Whip on medium speed until medium peaks form, 2 minutes.

10. When the custard is set, mound the whipped cream on top of the pie and swirl with a decorative swoosh. Top with the crushed malted milk balls. Slice and serve.

TASTY PRIDE

Lemon Poppyseed Crinkle Cookies

JUSTIN BURKE-SAMSON

**MAKES ABOUT
25 COOKIES**

½ cup (1 stick) unsalted
butter, softened

1 cup plus 2 tablespoons
granulated sugar

Zest of 2 lemons

Juice of 3 lemons

1 large egg

1 large egg yolk

½ teaspoon vanilla extract

2⅓ cups all-purpose flour

2 teaspoons baking
powder

½ teaspoon salt

2 tablespoons poppy seeds

Confectioners' sugar, for
dusting

I grew up with *The Golden Girls*, both literally and figuratively. My aunt lived in Arizona on the Colorado River and I spent my summers with her while my mom took a break from single parenthood. My aunt owned a ceramics business and ran painting classes out of her house. She had a regular weekly class of four women, senior in their years but far from elderly—and like *The Golden Girls* would, these women loved and supported me for who I was. They would gather around the table and paint and gossip, always while eating some type of dessert. Betty was the sweetest of them all. She was the baker in the group and always the one who brought dessert. To me, Betty was the queen of baking and the first person to introduce me to new flavors—ones that weren't common in the Arizona desert. Of everything she ever made, my favorite was lemon poppyseed bread, doused with icing. These cookies are in honor of Betty: they're moist, quick bread-like cookies punched with enough poppy seeds and lemon to remind you to always stay golden.

1. In the bowl of a stand mixer fitted with the paddle attachment, combine the butter, sugar, and lemon zest. Cream on medium-high speed for 5 minutes, until light and fluffy. Scrape down the sides of the bowl, then add the lemon juice, egg, egg yolk, and vanilla and mix on medium speed for 4 minutes, until fully incorporated. The mixture will look broken at first, but it will come together.

2. In a large bowl, whisk together the flour, baking powder, salt, and poppy seeds.

3. With the mixer on low speed, slowly add the dry ingredients to the wet ingredients and mix until just incorporated. Do not overmix. Finish mixing with a rubber spatula to incorporate any floury bits at the bottom of the bowl. Cover the bowl with plastic wrap and chill in the refrigerator for at least 2 hours and up to overnight.

4. Line 2 baking sheets with parchment paper. Use a 2-tablespoon cookie scoop to portion out the dough and place the balls on the pans at least 2 inches apart. Wrap the baking sheets in plastic wrap and freeze the dough for at least 2 hours or up to 1 month.

5. Preheat the oven to 350°F.

6. Roll the balls of cookie dough in confectioners' sugar, then return to the baking sheets. Bake the cookies for 16 minutes, rotating the pans halfway, or until cracks form and the edges are slightly golden. Remove the cookies from the oven and let cool slightly on the baking sheets. Transfer the cookies to a wire rack to cool completely before serving.

Oatmeal Raisin Cookie Ice Cream Sandwiches

EDD KIMBER

MAKES 12 ICE CREAM SANDWICHES

Oatmeal Raisin Cookies

1½ cups raisins

Boiling water, for soaking raisins

1½ cups all-purpose flour

1 teaspoon baking powder

½ teaspoon ground cinnamon

½ teaspoon kosher salt

2 tablespoons malt powder

1 cup (2 sticks) unsalted butter, room temperature

½ cup plus 2 tablespoons granulated sugar

½ cup plus 1 tablespoon packed light brown sugar

1 teaspoon vanilla extract

1 extra-large egg

2 cups old-fashioned rolled oats

Ice Cream

½ cup raisins

⅓ cup rum

2 pints vanilla ice cream, softened

Chocolate Shell

2 tablespoons coconut oil

1½ cups chopped dark chocolate, melted

A decade ago, I'd just found out I was going to be one of the bakers on the first-ever season of *The Great British Bake Off*. When I walked into that tent for the first time, I distinctly remember feeling self-conscious. Growing up, I was the awkward kid who didn't really have any friends and always felt out of place. I lost weight, hoping to shed that feeling, and I came out, hoping that would help, too—but it wasn't until I entered the world of food and found a career that made me incredibly happy that I started to feel comfortable in my own skin. After *Bake Off* finished, I began a new chapter with a new sense of self. I started making strides toward being happier with who I am and not caring which box or label I fit into. Now I'm more concerned with nurturing my own happiness. One way to do that? With ice cream sandwiches. This version, made with rum-soaked raisins and chewy oatmeal cookies, brings me joy both through the process of making them and, of course, through eating them. In an abstract way, this recipe is a simple reminder to always stay proud, happy, and confident with who I really am.

1. Make the cookies: Add the raisins to a small bowl. Cover with boiling water and let sit for 15 minutes to plump (this will also prevent the raisins from burning while baking). Drain the water, then let the raisins cool.

2. In a large bowl, mix the flour, baking powder, cinnamon, salt, and malt powder.

3. In the bowl of a stand mixer fitted with the paddle attachment, beat together the butter and sugars on medium speed until light and fluffy, about 5 minutes. Mix in the vanilla and egg.

4. Add the dry ingredients to the wet ingredients and mix until just combined. Add the oats and soaked raisins and mix until evenly distributed. Cover the bowl with plastic wrap and chill in the refrigerator for 2 hours.

5. Preheat the oven to 350°F. Line 2 baking sheets with parchment paper.

6. Using a 2-tablespoon cookie scoop, portion out the chilled dough, then roll into balls. Working in batches, place the dough balls on the prepared baking sheets, spacing about 2 inches apart. Bake for 12 to 14 minutes, or until golden around the edges but still a bit soft and pale in the center. Let the cookies cool completely.

7. Make the ice cream: In a small saucepan over low heat, combine the raisins and rum and bring to a boil. Once the rum is boiling, remove the pan from the heat and let cool.

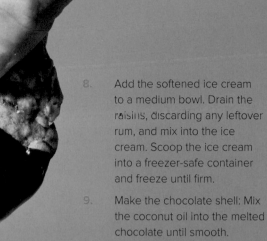

8. Add the softened ice cream to a medium bowl. Drain the raisins, discarding any leftover rum, and mix into the ice cream. Scoop the ice cream into a freezer-safe container and freeze until firm.

9. Make the chocolate shell: Mix the coconut oil into the melted chocolate until smooth.

10. To assemble, sandwich a small scoop of ice cream between 2 cookies. Dip the ice cream sandwiches halfway into the chocolate shell, then place on a baking sheet lined with parchment paper. Let sit for about 1 minute for the chocolate to set, then transfer to the freezer until ready to serve. (The sandwiches will keep in an airtight container in the freezer for up to 2 weeks.)

Strawberry Jalapeño Sundae
with Chocolate Ice Cream

DOUGLAS QUINT & BRYAN PETROFF

SERVES 4 TO 6

1 pound fresh strawberries, hulled and quartered

¼ cup sugar

2 jalapeños, seeded and minced, plus thinly sliced rounds for garnishing

1 cup cold water

4 tablespoons fresh lemon juice

2 tablespoons orange-flavored liqueur, such as Grand Marnier (optional)

1½ teaspoons grated lemon zest

Chocolate ice cream

We started Big Gay Ice Cream in a borrowed soft-serve truck that came with some inherent operating restrictions. From chocolate and spice to drag queens and astronauts, we learned how to create imaginative ice cream toppings that would later define our menu as we expanded the business. If it's a mismatch that somehow works when you pull it together, we're in. One thing that we particularly enjoy is marrying heat with unexpected flavor. Just as dark chocolate is better with a bit of chipotle chile added, many sweet, juicy fruits also become better when you kick them up with heat. In this recipe we combine strawberries and jalapeños, and in doing so, we boost the strawberry's flavor notes to surprising places. We love the topping over chocolate ice cream, but it's great on vanilla, strawberry, or whatever other flavor you want. Maybe try it over something unexpected and make a new combination! You know we'll be with you on that.

1. In a large bowl, toss together the strawberries and sugar. Cover with plastic wrap and refrigerate for at least 30 minutes and up to 8 hours.

2. In a small bowl, combine the jalapeños, cold water, and 2 tablespoons of the lemon juice and let sit at room temperature, uncovered, for 15 to 30 minutes. (The longer the jalapeños soak, the less heat they will have.) Drain using a fine-mesh sieve, discarding the liquid, and add to the strawberry mixture.

3. Add the remaining 2 tablespoons lemon juice and Grand Marnier, if using, to the strawberries, toss, and let sit at room temperature, uncovered, for 15 minutes.

4. Right before serving, add the lemon zest to the strawberry mixture and toss to combine. Spoon over scoops of chocolate ice cream, garnish with sliced jalapeños, and serve immediately.

Mexican Chocolate Corn Coffee Cake

IRVIN LIN

SERVES 12

Corn Milk and Mix-In

1 medium ear of corn, shucked

1½ cups half and half

½ cup granulated sugar

2 tablespoons cornstarch

2 teaspoons ground cinnamon

½ teaspoon kosher salt

Crumb Topping

1 cup all-purpose flour

⅔ cup packed dark brown sugar

¼ cup natural unsweetened cocoa powder

2 teaspoons ground cinnamon

¼ teaspoon cayenne

½ teaspoon kosher salt

½ cup (1 stick) unsalted butter, cold

Coffee Cake Batter

3 cups all-purpose flour

½ cup cornmeal

4 teaspoons baking powder

1 teaspoon kosher salt

1½ cups granulated sugar

½ cup (1 stick) unsalted butter, room temperature

2 teaspoons vanilla extract

2 large eggs

My partner, AJ, and I have always shared a goal of hitting all sixty-one national parks in the United States—so when he suggested that we go to Joshua Tree National Park one weekend, I didn't think anything of it. During our hike, we came to a rock formation, where AJ stood up and said, "I have a present for you." I immediately became suspicious; he is *not* one to spring surprises on me. As I tried to puzzle together what he was doing, he pulled out the gift from his backpack. It was a large photo album filled with pictures from the twenty-six parks we had already visited, and at the end of the book was the question "Will you marry me?" I obviously said yes, and after we'd made our way out of the park, we ended up at an ice cream shop in Palm Springs called Ice Cream & Shop(pe). We celebrated our engagement with a scoop each of Mexican chocolate and sweet corn ice cream, an oddball flavor combination that worked so well I turned it into a coffee cake in honor of that day. You can eat this cake for breakfast, for dessert, or to celebrate any of life's big moments.

1. Make the corn milk and mix-in: Add the ear of corn and half and half to a large pot and bring to a boil over medium-high heat. Reduce the heat to low, cover, and simmer for 8 minutes, until the corn is tender.

2. Remove the corn and let it cool to the touch, then cut the kernels off the cob into a medium bowl and set aside. Return the cob to the pot with the half and half, cover, and set aside to steep for 30 minutes.

3. Add the sugar, cornstarch, cinnamon, and salt to the bowl with the corn kernels. Toss to coat and set aside.

4. Make the crumb topping: Add the flour, brown sugar, cocoa powder, cinnamon, cayenne, and salt to a medium bowl. Cut the cold butter into ½-inch cubes and add to the dry ingredients. Using your fingertips, toss the butter to coat, then press the butter into small, pea-sized bits. Chill in the refrigerator until ready to use.

5. Preheat the oven to 350°F. Grease a 9 by 13-inch baking dish with nonstick spray.

6. Make the batter: Put the flour, cornmeal, baking powder, and salt in a large bowl and whisk to combine.

7. Add the sugar, butter, and vanilla to the bowl of a stand mixer fitted with the paddle attachment. Cream until fluffy and light in color, about 3 minutes. Add the eggs, one at a time, mixing until fully incorporated before adding the next. Scrape down the sides of the bowl with a spatula as needed.

8. Measure out the corn-infused half and half; you should have about 1¼ cups. Discard the cob.

9. Add half the dry ingredients to the stand mixer and mix to incorporate. Add half the corn-infused half and half and stir to combine. Repeat with the remaining ingredients. Fold the corn mix-in into the batter with a rubber spatula. Pour the batter into the prepared pan and spread in an even layer. Sprinkle the crumb topping on top.

10. Bake for 40 to 50 minutes, until a toothpick inserted in the center comes out clean. Let the cake cool, then slice into 12 squares.

Whiskey-Glazed Doughnuts

ILIANA REGAN

MAKES 12 DOUGHNUTS

Doughnuts

2 packages active dry yeast

1 cup milk, heated to 110–115°F

4 cups high-gluten flour or bread flour, plus more for dusting

½ cup granulated sugar

1 tablespoon kosher salt

½ cup sourdough starter, or scant ½ cup whole wheat flour

3 large eggs, room temperature

1 large egg white, room temperature

1½ tablespoons vanilla extract

1 vanilla bean, seeds scraped

¾ cup (1½ sticks) unsalted butter, melted and cooled

6 to 8 cups canola oil, plus more for greasing

Glaze

1 cup whiskey

3 cups confectioners' sugar

I'm pretty humble when it comes to just about everything, and I hate being the center of attention. My voice is soft and quiet. Most of the time, I'd rather you not hear me, see me, or try to talk to me. I like to disappear, living in the woods far away from everyone other than my wife and dogs. But there are a few things I *won't* be quiet about—like the pride I have in being married to my wonderful wife, and the pride I have in perfecting my whiskey-glazed doughnuts recipe—so much so that I strut around my bakery like a damn peacock showing them off. When someone says to me that these doughnuts are good, I say, "I know." I even give them to customers who visit my bakery and *don't* order one, just so they can taste how good they are. I eat a couple a day and can confidently say I make the best doughnuts I've ever had.

1. In a small bowl, stir the yeast into the milk; let sit for 5 minutes, until foamy.

2. In the bowl of a stand mixer fitted with the dough hook, combine the flour, sugar, and salt. Add the starter and mix. Add the yeast mixture and mix on medium-low to combine. With the mixer running, add the eggs, egg white, vanilla, and vanilla seeds. Add the melted butter and mix until incorporated. Increase speed to medium-high and mix until the dough is extremely tacky, 8 minutes. Transfer the dough to a large greased bowl. Cover and let rest in the refrigerator for 24 hours.

3. Turn the dough out onto a lightly floured surface and roll out to a ¼-inch thickness. Cut out doughnuts using a 4-inch round cutter and use a 1-inch round cutter to cut out the centers. Set the doughnuts on a lightly greased baking sheet. Gather any excess dough, let rest for 10 minutes, then reroll to cut out more doughnuts. You should have about 12 total. Cover the doughnuts with plastic wrap and let proof for 1 hour and 20 minutes, or until puffy and just barely doubled in size. Transfer to the refrigerator to cool slightly, until they are between 55°F and 70°F.

4. Make the glaze: Add the whiskey to a medium pan set over medium-high heat and cook until just starting to bubble around the edges. Remove the pan from the heat. With a long match, carefully ignite the whiskey in the pan. Do not disturb until the flames have burned off. Let cool.

5. Transfer the whiskey to a large bowl and whisk in the confectioners' sugar, ¼ cup at a time, until the glaze falls in smooth ribbons from the whisk.

6. Heat the canola oil in a large heavy-bottomed pot until it reaches 320°F to 340°F. Working in batches, fry the doughnuts in the hot oil for 1 minute on the first side. Flip and fry for another 2 minutes, then flip again and fry for 1 minute more, until golden brown. Transfer to a wire rack to cool slightly. Dip one side of the doughnuts in the glaze, then return to the wire rack to let any excess glaze drip off. Serve warm.

Blueberry Gooey Butter Cake

APRIL ANDERSON

SERVES 18

Base

1½ cups all-purpose flour

1 cup granulated sugar

¼ cup dry milk powder

1½ teaspoons baking powder

½ teaspoon kosher salt

¾ cup (1½ sticks) unsalted butter, ½ cup cubed and chilled, and ¼ cup melted

1½ teaspoons vanilla extract

1 large egg

Filling

1 (8-ounce) package cream cheese, softened

2 large eggs

2 teaspoons lemon extract

Zest of 1 lemon

5 cups sifted confectioners' sugar, plus more for dusting

1 cup fresh blueberries

Two years after Michelle and I met and started dating, we headed to St. Louis to join her family at their annual reunion. It was our first time traveling there together. We were excited to be with a family who accepted and loved us as a couple—but also stoked because we had recently read a story that claimed St. Louis was the birthplace of gooey butter cake. Michelle and I love trying new foods together, so at our first opportunity, we took a break from family time to track down a slice of the stuff. After our first bites, we fell in love a second time; I wanted to re-create that experience once we got back home to show my love and appreciation for my wife. I scoured the internet in search of the perfect recipe. Every version I found used boxed cake mix as the base, but I wanted to create it from scratch. It took two years of trying and failing to devise the perfect formula. When we opened our bakery together in 2013, we knew the dessert we fell in love over had to be on the menu. Sharing this recipe with our customers is our way of sharing the love we have for each other.

1. Preheat the oven to 350°F. Grease a 9 by 13-inch baking dish with nonstick spray. Line with parchment paper, leaving overhang on the short sides so it's easy to lift out the cake after baking.

2. Make the base: In the bowl of a stand mixer fitted with the paddle attachment, combine the flour, sugar, milk powder, baking powder, salt, and ½ cup chilled butter. Mix on medium speed until the butter breaks down to small, pea-sized pieces, about 2 minutes. Add the vanilla, ¼ cup melted butter, and the egg and mix to incorporate. Transfer to the prepared baking dish and spread in an even layer using clean hands sprayed with nonstick spray. Transfer to the freezer. Clean the stand mixer bowl and paddle.

3. Make the filling: In the bowl of the stand mixer fitted with the paddle attachment, combine the cream cheese and eggs. Beat on medium speed for 4 to 5 minutes, scraping down the sides of the bowl halfway, until pale yellow but still chunky. Add the lemon extract and zest and mix on medium-high speed for 5 to 7 minutes, scraping down the sides of the bowl occasionally, until the filling is completely smooth. With the mixer running on low speed, add the confectioners' sugar, a third at a time, and continue mixing until there are no lumps. Gently fold in the blueberries with a rubber spatula. Pour the filling over the base and spread in an even layer.

4. Bake the cake for 45 to 50 minutes, until the top is lightly golden. Let the cake cool for at least 2 hours, lift the cake out of the pan, then dust the top with confectioners' sugar and slice into 18 pieces.

Saffron and Pistachio Shortbread Cookies

JESSE SZEWCZYK

MAKES 24 COOKIES

1 cup (2 sticks) unsalted butter

¾ teaspoon saffron threads, lightly crushed with your fingers

2 cups all-purpose flour, plus more for dusting

¼ teaspoon baking powder

¼ teaspoon kosher salt

¾ cup sifted confectioners' sugar

2 teaspoons vanilla extract

1 teaspoon almond extract

6 ounces semisweet chocolate, chopped

1 tablespoon coconut oil or vegetable shortening

¾ cup finely chopped roasted and salted pistachios

Flaky sea salt (optional)

My mother always loved baking and was willing to travel out of her way for quality ingredients. There was a Middle Eastern market she was fond of in downtown Chicago, about two hours from our house in the sleepy suburbs. We would drive out there every few months to stock up on various ingredients—and I would be excited every time. Part of why I loved going there was that it was near Boys Town, Chicago's gayborhood. Those colorful city blocks were the only place I ever saw queer people out and about. My mother would stock up on saffron, pistachios, and other treats, and I would snack on our drive home as I stared out the window at queer folks laughing, holding hands, and doing nothing other than being 100 percent authentically themselves. This outward expression of pride and happiness became a goal for me. When I graduated college, I moved in just a few blocks from the heart of Boys Town. Whenever I bake with saffron, the sweet scent reminds me just how far I've come.

1. Melt the butter in a small pot over medium heat. Add the saffron and cook, stirring until the butter turns bright orange and is fragrant, about 2 minutes. Pour the butter into a heatproof bowl, cover with plastic wrap, and let cool in the refrigerator for 1 hour, until solid.

2. Preheat the oven to 350°F. Line 2 baking sheets with parchment paper.

3. In a medium bowl, sift together the flour, baking powder, and salt and set aside.

4. Add the cooled butter and confectioners' sugar to the bowl of a stand mixer fitted with the paddle attachment. Beat on medium speed until light and fluffy, about 2 minutes. Add the vanilla and almond extracts and beat just until incorporated. Add the flour mixture and mix on low speed until a dry dough forms, about 1 minute.

5. Transfer the dough to a lightly floured surface and press together into a ball. Dust the top of the dough with flour and roll into a ½-inch-thick circle. Using a 1½-inch round cookie cutter, cut out cookies and place on the prepared baking sheets, spacing about 1 inch apart. Prick the tops with a fork 3 times and freeze for 10 minutes.

6. Bake the cookies until lightly golden brown, 14 to 16 minutes. Let cool completely on the baking sheets.

7. Put the chocolate and coconut oil in a medium microwave-safe bowl. Microwave in 10-second increments, stirring between each, until the chocolate is completely melted and smooth. Dip half of each cookie in the melted chocolate, then roll the edge in the pistachios. Sprinkle with flaky sea salt, if desired. Set the dipped cookies on a piece of parchment paper and let set for 1 hour before serving.

Dark Chocolate Mousse Cake

BILL YOSSES

SERVES 10

Chocolate Sponge Cake

6 large eggs

6 large egg yolks

1 cup granulated sugar

1 teaspoon vanilla extract

1 cup all-purpose flour, sifted

3 tablespoons unsweetened dark cocoa powder

Filling

4 tablespoons (½ stick) unsalted butter

2⅓ cups chopped semisweet chocolate

2 large pasteurized eggs, separated

2 teaspoons instant coffee

¼ cup plus 1 tablespoon dark rum

3 tablespoons praline paste or chocolate-hazelnut spread

Pinch of kosher salt

2 tablespoons granulated sugar

1⅓ cups heavy cream

2 tablespoons confectioners' sugar

This celebratory cake always reminds me of the incredible day in 2012 when President Obama voiced his support for same-sex marriage. I was lucky enough to be the White House executive pastry chef at that time, and I remember the absolute thrill I felt. It was the first time a U.S. president had ever said this, and the sentiment sent shockwaves of joy through the LGBTQ+ community. Anyone who grew up gay has felt the need to be invisible at times, to avoid the stigma associated with being different, and now the leader of the free world had said it out loud: that all Americans should be treated as equal. Three years later, the U.S. Supreme Court ruled in favor of same-sex marriage. This dessert, a simple chocolate cake that can be dressed up or down however you like, is fit for a birthday, a party, or a political triumph.

1. Preheat the oven to 375°F. Grease and line three 9-inch round cake pans with parchment paper (work in batches if needed).

2. Make the cake: In a double boiler or heatproof bowl set over a small pot of gently simmering water, combine the eggs, egg yolks, sugar, and vanilla. Cook, stirring constantly, until the eggs are warm to the touch, 4 to 5 minutes. Remove the double boiler from the heat.

3. Beat the egg mixture with an electric mixer on medium-high speed until pale yellow and tripled in volume, about 7 minutes. Sift in the flour and cocoa powder, then fold in with a rubber spatula to incorporate. Divide the batter evenly among the prepared cake pans.

4. Bake for 8 to 10 minutes or until a tester inserted in the center of a cake comes out clean. Let cool completely.

5. Make the filling: In a double boiler or heatproof bowl set over a small pot of gently simmering water, melt the butter and chocolate until smooth. Remove from the heat and let cool slightly.

6. Meanwhile, in a large bowl, mix the egg yolks, instant coffee, rum, and praline paste until smooth. Whisk in the melted chocolate mixture.

7. In a medium bowl, beat the egg whites and salt with an electric hand mixer until soft peaks form. With the mixer running, gradually add the granulated sugar and continue beating until the mixture reaches stiff peaks.

8. In a separate medium bowl, beat the cream and confectioners' sugar with an electric hand mixer until soft peaks form.

9. Using a rubber spatula, carefully fold the meringue into the chocolate mixture, followed by the whipped cream, taking care not to deflate the egg whites.

10. Grease a 9-inch springform pan with nonstick spray. Line the sides with parchment paper.

11. Add a layer of cake to the bottom of the springform pan. Top with about one-third of the filling and spread in an even layer. Repeat with the remaining cakes and filling, finishing with a layer of filling. Wrap the springform with plastic wrap and refrigerate for at least 8 hours.

12. To serve, release the springform and remove the parchment paper. Slice with a hot knife.

TASTY PRIDE

Chocolate Chip Cookie Skillet à la Mode

NATASHA CASE & FREYA ESTRELLER

SERVES 8

½ cup (1 stick) unsalted butter, cubed

1 cup packed dark brown sugar

2 teaspoons vanilla extract

1 large egg

1¼ cups all-purpose flour

½ teaspoon kosher salt

½ teaspoon baking powder

¼ teaspoon baking soda

½ cup semisweet chocolate chips

Vanilla ice cream

In 2009, we launched the ice cream brand Coolhaus, which has become kind of famous for its ice cream sandwiches. Within the same week, we started making ice cream and cookies from scratch *and* we started dating. It has been an incredibly romantic way to get to know each other. I mean, driving a beat-up old ice cream truck into the sunset, headed to a wedding in Malibu—it was perfect.

We love this decadent recipe for how it creates a perfectly soft but chewy skillet cookie that is all about sharing and uniting folks over a common good. You can enjoy it for any occasion: a dinner party, a birthday celebration, or even an after-school snack. It is especially delicious served hot—and it is the perfect platform for any flavor of ice cream, though we love vanilla.

1. Preheat the oven to 350°F.

2. Heat a 9-inch cast-iron skillet over medium-low heat. Melt the butter in the skillet and swirl to coat the bottom and sides. Remove the skillet from the heat and let cool until the butter is melted but just barely warm, about 5 minutes.

3. Add the brown sugar, vanilla, and egg to the skillet and stir using a wooden spoon until any large chunks of sugar are dissolved and the mixture is completely smooth. Add the flour, salt, baking powder, and baking soda and stir until just combined. Do not overmix.

4. Add half the chocolate chips and stir to evenly distribute. Spread the dough in the skillet in an even layer and wipe off any cookie dough or flour stuck to the sides. Top with the remaining chocolate chips.

5. Bake until slightly golden but still gooey in the middle, about 20 minutes. Remove from the oven and top with ice cream. Serve immediately.

Wedding Cake Cookie Sandwiches

BRIAN HART HOFFMAN

MAKES 15 COOKIE SANDWICHES

Cookies

1 cup (2 sticks) unsalted butter, softened

2 cups granulated sugar

2 large eggs, room temperature

1 tablespoon vanilla paste or extract

½ teaspoon almond extract

2¼ cups all-purpose flour

¾ cup bread flour

2 teaspoons baking powder

2 teaspoons cream of tartar

1 teaspoon baking soda

1 teaspoon kosher salt

2 tablespoons whole milk

1 cup sprinkles, plus more for topping

Wedding Cake Buttercream

½ cup (1 stick) unsalted butter, softened

1 (2-pound) box confectioners' sugar, sifted

¾ cup whole milk

1 teaspoon almond extract

As a child, I loved weddings and went to as many as I could. My mom was the church organist, my aunt Janice was a wedding coordinator, and my aunt Cheryl loved a good slice of cake. As I grew up and realized I was gay, my love for weddings faded. How could I love something I wouldn't be able to have myself? It saddened me to think that I wouldn't be able to celebrate my future love and my future husband along with my *own* wedding cake, so I became comfortable on team "I don't need a wedding to be in love, so I don't want one." Then I met Stephen. And I wanted one. After a trip to Seattle to get legally married in the courthouse (this was in 2013, two years before the nationwide ruling), we had our dream wedding at my mom's house in Alabama on a bluff at sunset, surrounded by 150 people who love us—complete with my dream wedding cake. This recipe is the flavor of that cake, with rainbow sprinkles added. Now a celebration is never too far from reach.

1. Make the cookies: In the bowl of a stand mixer fitted with the paddle attachment, beat the butter and 1⅓ cups sugar on medium speed until fluffy, 3 to 4 minutes. Add the eggs, one at a time, beating well after each addition. Beat in the vanilla paste and almond extract.

2. In a medium bowl, whisk together the flours, baking powder, cream of tartar, baking soda, and salt. With the mixer running on low speed, gradually add the dry ingredients to the wet ingredients, beating until just combined. Add the milk and beat to incorporate. Stir in the sprinkles until distributed. Cover the bowl with plastic wrap and refrigerate for at least 1 hour or up to 3 days.

3. Preheat the oven to 350°F. Line 4 baking sheets, or as many as you have, with parchment paper.

4. Using a 1½-inch cookie scoop, portion out the dough and roll into balls. Roll the balls in the remaining ⅔ cup sugar. Place them 3 inches apart on the prepared baking sheets. Top with more sprinkles, if desired. Bake until the edges are lightly browned, 12 to 14 minutes. Let the cookies cool on the pans for 5 minutes, then transfer to wire racks.

5. While the cookies cool, make the buttercream: In the bowl of a stand mixer fitted with a paddle attachment, beat the butter at medium speed until creamy, 3 to 4 minutes. Gradually add the confectioners' sugar and milk, beating until the buttercream reaches a spreadable consistency. Add the almond extract and beat until combined, about 4 minutes.

6. Transfer the buttercream to a piping bag fitted with a large star piping tip or a zippered plastic bag with a corner snipped off. Pipe the buttercream in a swirl onto the flat sides of half the cookies. Sandwich with the remaining cookies.

TASTY PRIDE

Lemon Ricotta Torta

RITA SODI & JODY WILLIAMS

MAKES ONE 9-INCH CAKE

2½ cups almond flour

½ cup all-purpose flour

1 cup (2 sticks) unsalted butter, softened

1½ cups granulated sugar

6 large eggs, separated

Zest of 7 lemons, preferably Meyer (about 14 teaspoons)

Juice of 3 lemons, preferably Meyer (about 6 tablespoons)

Scant 1¼ cups ricotta cheese

Boiling water

Confectioners' sugar

Fresh herbs or flowers

We made this lemon ricotta cake together on our wedding day in 2015 in New York City. We dusted the cake with confectioners' sugar and garnished it with fresh herbs, flowering thyme, mint, and lavender—and we even saved a bouquet of the herbs to dry as a keepsake. We continue to make this popular cake in the spring with Meyer lemons and fresh ricotta in our restaurants. It will always be nicknamed "the wedding cake" between the two of us, even though the menu simply lists it as a lemon ricotta cake. It's simple and can be dressed up or down with herbs or confectioners' sugar, or served all by itself for a rustic dessert fit for a wedding.

1. Preheat the oven to 325°F. Line a 9-inch springform pan with parchment paper and wrap the outside of the pan with foil.

2. In a medium bowl, combine the almond flour and all-purpose flour. Set aside.

3. In a large bowl, beat the butter and sugar with an electric hand mixer until smooth and light, about 3 minutes. One at a time, add the egg yolks, followed by the lemon zest and juice. Fold in the flour mixture. Gently fold in the ricotta.

4. In a separate large bowl, whip the egg whites with an electric hand mixer until soft peaks form. Fold the egg whites into the batter, making sure not to overmix.

5. Pour the batter into the prepared springform pan. Set the pan in a shallow baking dish. Pour 1 to 2 inches of boiling water into the baking dish; the foil will prevent the water from seeping into the cake. Bake until the cake is set in the middle and just beginning to brown, 60 to 70 minutes. Remove the cake from the oven and let cool completely before removing the springform pan.

6. Decorate the cake with confectioners' sugar and herbs and flowers, as desired, before slicing and serving.

Green Tea Cake
with Strawberry Semifreddo

PICHET ONG

SERVES 8

Green Tea Cake

2 teaspoons loose green tea, preferably Sencha

¼ cup whole milk

¼ cup sour cream

1 tablespoon plus 1 teaspoon grapeseed oil

1 teaspoon kosher salt

⅔ cup sugar

1 large egg

⅓ cup cornstarch

⅓ cup rice flour

1 teaspoon baking soda

¼ cup matcha powder

Strawberry Semifreddo

1 pint fresh strawberries, hulled and halved, plus more for garnish

¼ cup plus 2 tablespoons sugar

3 large eggs

2 large egg yolks

Zest and juice of 1 lemon

2½ cups heavy whipping cream, cold

During my two decades working in the food industry, I've been happy to witness a growing sense of acceptance inside the kitchens. Now more than ever, I can be my authentic self at work. As a pastry chef, I am also able to express myself through my desserts—through seasonal produce, different textures, and temperatures. In this semifreddo recipe (which is just a fancy name for a somewhat frozen dessert), strawberries are cooked down and folded into whipped cream and cooked eggs to produce a light-as-a-feather base that then gets frozen—almost like strawberry ice cream. This mixture is layered with a homemade green tea cake to contrast the sweetness of the strawberries, creating an impressive dessert that can be made ahead of time and sliced when ready to eat. It's an elegant cake that is fairly simple to pull off, especially if you bake the layers the day before assembling.

1. Make the cake: Preheat the oven to 350°F. Line two 9 by 13-inch baking sheets with parchment paper.

2. In a small pot, bring 1 cup of water to a bare simmer. Add the loose tea and transfer to a tall, narrow container, such as a cup, then blend with an immersion blender until the tea is finely ground. Strain and return to the container. Add the milk, sour cream, grapeseed oil, salt, sugar, and egg and use the immersion blender to process until smooth.

3. In a medium bowl, sift together the cornstarch, rice flour, baking soda, and matcha. Add the dry ingredients to the wet ingredients and pulse with the immersion blender until the batter is smooth with no lumps.

4. Divide the batter evenly between the prepared baking sheets and spread out to the edges. Bake for 8 to 10 minutes, rotating halfway, until a tester inserted in the center comes out clean. Remove from the oven and let cool completely.

5. Make the semifreddo: In a medium pot over medium heat, combine the strawberries with 2 tablespoons of the sugar. Stir every 5 minutes, until thickened, 20 minutes total. The texture should be jamlike and reach about 208°F. Remove the pot from the heat and let cool.

6. In a double boiler or large bowl set over a pot of simmering water, combine the eggs, egg yolks, remaining ¼ cup sugar, and the lemon zest and juice. Cook, whisking constantly, until the sugar is dissolved, the mixture is slightly thickened, and the temperature reaches 155°F, about 5 minutes.

7. Transfer the egg mixture to the bowl of a stand mixer fitted with the whisk attachment. Whip on high speed until almost tripled in volume and the bottom of the bowl is cool, about 6 minutes.

8. Fold the strawberry mixture into the egg mixture until well combined. Transfer the mixture to a separate large bowl, set aside, and wash the stand mixer bowl.

9. Add the heavy cream to the clean bowl and place it back on the mixer fitted with the whisk attachment. Whip on high speed until soft peaks form, about 30 seconds. Add half the whipped cream to the egg mixture and stir to combine, then gently fold in the remaining whipped cream until just incorporated.

10. To assemble the cake, line a 9 by 4-inch loaf pan with parchment paper, leaving some to overhang on the long sides. Lightly grease with nonstick spray, then line with a sheet of plastic wrap so there are 4 inches of overhang on all sides. Set the pan in the refrigerator while you prepare the cake.

11. Cut one sheet of cake crosswise into 8 pieces, each about 1½ inches wide. Cut half of the second sheet of cake crosswise into four 1½-inch-wide pieces so you have 12 total pieces of cake. (Leftover cake can be used to patch any gaps during assembly.)

12. Remove the mold from the refrigerator. Add a layer of strawberry semifreddo, about ½ inch thick. Top with 2 cake strips. Continue layering the remaining ingredients, finishing with a layer of semifreddo. When finished, gently tap the pan on a flat surface to fill in trapped air pockets and even out the top. Wrap the plastic wrap over the semifreddo, pressing it directly against the surface. Freeze the cake overnight to set.

13. When ready to serve, remove the cake from the pan and unwrap. Slice crosswise into 8 pieces, each about 1 inch thick. Plate each slice and garnish with strawberries.

Acknowledgments

This cookbook is the direct result of the LGBTQ+ community joining forces with passionate allies. From the editors to the art directors to the legal teams who worked tirelessly to make this book the best it could possibly be, thank you. It's allies like yourselves who show the world that equality is not just an LGBTQ+ issue, but a human rights issue.

Jesse would like to thank:

Tasty, for taking a firm stance on equality and being dedicated to inclusiveness and representation in mainstream food media. Thank you for providing the platform, resources, support, and guidance needed to make this cookbook a success—and, of course, for your generous donation to GLAAD. And to Emily DePaula, Talia Halperin, and Eric Karp for spearheading the project.

The greater BuzzFeed team, for all of your help. From the talented team of copy editors (Emmy Favilla, Miranda Kantor, and Sarah Schweppe) to the endlessly helpful finance team (Jake Raphaelson and Rikki McKernan) to the legal team who showed so much patience (Ashley Tan and Wajmah Yaqubi), I could not have done this without each and every one of you. Thank you for jumping in with so much love, enthusiasm, and dedication.

Everyone at Penguin Random House—especially Amanda Englander—for making sure this book was a true celebration of our community. Mark McCauslin, Mia Johnson, Stephanie Huntwork, Kim Tyner, Nick Patton, Stephanie Davis, and David Hawk: You took my vision and made it more than I could have ever imagined. Thank you for taking a chance and believing in this project, and for your generous donation to GLAAD.

The amazing photo team who turned this project into a true work of art. Thank you to Lauren Volo, Monica Pierini, Maeve Sheridan, Krystal Rack, and Andie McMahon for sharing your talents. Watching the recipes and stories be translated into such stunning photos has been the highlight of my career. You cooked and styled with so much love and passion, and I cannot think of a better and more talented team to have tackled this project with. Thank you.

Danielle Daitch, for working tirelessly to make sure every recipe was delicious, reliable, and the best it could possibly be. You were a blessing to this project, and words can't express how much your support meant to me.

Thank you, Sophie Peoples, for designing a book as colorful, beautiful, and vibrant as the community itself.

GLAAD. You are the ones doing the hard work, and I cannot thank you enough for your tireless efforts and dedication to making the world a more loving and accepting place for members of the LGBTQ+ community. Your work toward accelerating acceptance is so important, and I am honored to have met you.

Equity at the Table, an online database of women and gender-nonconforming folks who work in food. This tool was an invaluable resource during the production of this book, and I am so thankful it exists.

My chosen food family, for always being there to answer questions, make introductions, and provide endless love and support. Your texts, emails, and late-night phone calls meant the world to me as I worked on this book. I love you all so much and am honored to call you my friends.

And, most important, all of the amazing contributors who made this book possible. I am forever grateful for the work the community has put into this book, and I hope you are all as proud of it as I am. Working with each and every one of you has been a dream come true. I am truly honored to be part of this community.

Contributor Bios

AARON HUTCHERSON is a freelance food writer, editor, and recipe developer based in New York City. He is the founder of the food blog *The Hungry Hutch* and has had recipes featured in numerous publications, including *New York Times Cooking*, *The Washington Post*, and *Jarry*.

ALANA McMILLAN & SABRINA CHEN are the cofounders of JaynesBeard, a monthly private supper club for lesbian and queer women. The event highlights up-and-coming, mostly queer female chefs and bartenders and is held at various locations throughout New York City.

ALEX KOONES is a private caterer and the chef and organizer of Babetown, a Brooklyn, New York—based supper club for queer, nonbinary, and trans individuals. She has worked in several celebrated restaurants, including NoMad, Jean-Georges, and The Breslin.

AMELIA RAMPE is a food stylist, writer, and recipe developer based in New York City. Her work has been featured in publications such as *Food52*, *Bon Appétit*, and *Epicurious*.

ANDRE SPRINGER (A.K.A SHAQUANDA) is the founder of Shaquanda's Hot Pepper Sauce, an artisan hot sauce company based in East Harlem, New York, that combines drag and hot sauce into one fiery (and delicious) package.

ANDY BARAGHANI is a senior food editor for *Bon Appétit* and *Healthyish* based in New York City. He has worked in several renowned restaurants, including Chez Panisse and Corton.

ANITA LO is the former chef and owner of the now-closed Michelin-starred restaurant Annisa in New York City. She is the author of two cookbooks— *Solo: A Modern Cookbook for a Party of One* and *Cooking Without Borders*— and was named one of *Food & Wine*'s Best New Chefs in America in 2001. She has been nominated for the James Beard Foundation's Best Chef of New York City award several times.

ANTONI POROWSKI is the food and wine expert on Netflix's Emmy Award—winning series *Queer Eye*, co-owner of Village Den restaurant in New York City, and author of *Antoni in the Kitchen*.

APRIL ANDERSON is the chef and co-owner of Good Cakes and Bakes, an organic community-oriented bakery located in Detroit.

ARNOLD MYINT is the chef/owner of several restaurants in Nashville (including BLVD Nashville) and was a contestant on *Top Chef* and *Food Network Star*. His drag persona, Suzy Wong, has hosted parties for charitable organizations such as the Trevor Project, Nashville Cares, and NOH8.

ART SMITH is a restaurant owner, author of multiple cookbooks, and the former personal chef for Oprah Winfrey. He is the founder of Common Threads, a nonprofit organization based in Chicago, which teaches children, families, and teachers how to cook healthy and accessible meals.

BEN MIMS is the Cooking Columnist for the *Los Angeles Times* and author of two cookbooks: *Air Fry Every Day* and *Sweet & Southern: Classic Desserts with a Twist*. He has worked at *Lucky Peach*, *Saveur*, and *Food & Wine* and was the pastry chef for Bar Agricole in San Francisco.

BILL SMITH is the author of *Seasoned in the South: Recipes from Crook's Corner and from Home*, which was named a *New York Times* Notable Book, a *Food & Wine* Best Book, and One of 10 Cookbooks Every Southerner Should Own by *Southern Living*. He has been nominated for the James Beard Foundation's Best Chef of the Southeast award and is the former executive chef for the beloved restaurant Crook's Corner in Chapel Hill, North Carolina.

BILL YOSSES is the owner of Perfect Pie in New York, author of multiple cookbooks (including *The Sweet Spot: Dialing Back Sugar and Amping Up Flavor*), and the former White House executive pastry chef. He was nicknamed The Crust Master by President Barack Obama and inducted into the James Beard Foundation's Who's Who of Food & Beverage in America in 2013.

BO DURHAM is the pastry chef of Mindy's HotChocolate Bakery in Chicago.

BRIAN HART HOFFMAN is the president and chief creative officer of Hoffman Media and the founder and editor in chief of *Bake from Scratch* magazine, based in Birmingham, Alabama.

BRYAN PETROFF & DOUGLAS QUINT are cofounders of Big Gay Ice Cream and authors of *Big Gay Ice Cream: Saucy Stories & Frozen Treats: Going All the Way with Ice Cream*.

CASEY ELSASS is a freelance food writer, author of *Maple Syrup*, and founder of Bushwick Kitchen, a Brooklyn-based sweet and spicy condiment company. His work has been featured in such publications as *Munchies*, *Epicurious*, and *Food52*.

CHARLIE MONLOUIS-ANDERLE is a freelance chef, full-spectrum doula, and co-chef of Yardy, a culinary events company focused on making meaningful stories through food and art.

DEBORAH VANTRECE & LORRAINE LANE are the co-owners of Twisted Soul Cookhouse & Pours, a contemporary soul food restaurant in Atlanta that has been featured on Food Network and was voted the Best New Restaurant in Atlanta by *The Georgia Voice*.

DIANA YEN is the founder of The Jewels of New York, a styling and culinary consulting studio in New York City, and author of *A Simple Feast: A Year of Stories and Recipes to Savor and Share*. Her work has been featured in such publications as *Food & Wine*, *Kinfolk*, and *Martha Stewart Living*.

EDD KIMBER is a London-based baker, food writer, and winner of the first season of *The Great British Bake Off*. He is the author of three cookbooks: *Patisserie Made Simple*, *Say It with Cake*, and *The Boy Who Bakes*. His work has been featured in several publications, including *BBC Good Food*, *Olive*, and *Bake from Scratch*.

ELAZAR SONTAG is a food writer based in Brooklyn, New York, and author of *Flavors of Oakland: A Cookbook in 20 Stories*. His work has been featured in publications such as the *Washington Post*, *Bon Appétit*, *New York* magazine, *Munchies*, and *Serious Eats*.

ELISE KORNACK & ANNA HIERONIMUS are the former co-owners of the now-closed Michelin-starred restaurant Take Root in Brooklyn. In 2016 they were named to *Forbes'* 30 Under 30 for Food & Drink. They currently live in the Catskills region of New York.

ELIZABETH FALKNER is a consulting chef and author of *Elizabeth Falkner's Demolition Desserts: Recipes from Citizen Cake* and *Cooking Off the Clock: Recipes from My Downtime*. She has appeared on numerous television shows, including *Top Chef Masters* and *The Next Iron Chef: Super Chefs*. In 2005 she was nominated for the James Beard Foundation's Best Pastry Chef award and received the Human Rights Campaign's Charles M. Holmes Award.

ELLE SIMONE SCOTT is the first black woman to star on *America's Test Kitchen* and is the founder of SheChef, a social enterprise that empowers women of color working in the culinary industry.

ERIC KIM is the senior editor and Table for One columnist at *Food52*. He was formerly the digital manager of FoodNetwork.com and a writing instructor at Columbia University.

FRANCES TARIGA-WESHNAK is the former executive chef of Megu in New York City and was a contestant on Season 3 of *Top Chef*.

GABRIELLA VIGOREAUX is a catering chef based in Winter Haven, Florida. She was previously the culinary director for Smith Canteen in Brooklyn and has developed recipes for several media outlets, including *Good Housekeeping* and *Women's Day*.

HANNAH HART is the star of the hit YouTube series *My Drunk Kitchen*, author of the *New York Times* bestselling memoir *Buffering: Unshared Tales of a Life Fully Loaded*, and author of two cookbooks, *My Drunk Kitchen* and *My Drunk Kitchen Holidays!* In 2017 she starred in her own Food Network miniseries, *I Hart Food*.

ILIANA REGAN is the chef and owner of the Michelin-starred restaurant Elizabeth in Chicago and author of *Burn the Place: A Memoir*. She was nominated for the James Beard Foundation's Best Chef Great Lakes award in 2018 and was named one of *Food & Wine*'s Best New Chefs in 2016.

IRVIN LIN is an IACP award–winning photographer, founder of the popular food blog *Eat the Love*, and author of *Marbled, Swirled, and Layered: 150 Recipes and Variations for Artful Bars, Cookies, Pies, Cakes, and More*.

JAKE COHEN is the editorial and test kitchen director for The Feedfeed and author of the upcoming cookbook *JEW-ISH*. He was previously the food critic for *Time Out New York* and the food editor for *Tasting Table* and has cooked in several celebrated restaurants, including ABC Kitchen in New York City.

JAMES PARK is a recipe developer and digital food personality based in New York City. He is a social media associate for *Eater*, acting as the site's "official eater."

JESSE SZEWCZYK is a recipe developer, food writer, and stylist based in New York City. His work has appeared in such publications as *BuzzFeed*, *The Kitchen*, *Food52*, and *Bake from Scratch*.

JESSE TYLER FERGUSON is an actor best known for his role as Mitchell on ABC's *Modern Family*. He is the cofounder of the food blog *Julie & Jesse* and of Tie the Knot, a nonprofit charity that sells limited-edition bow ties with proceeds donated toward organizations fighting for LGBTQ+ rights.

JESSICA BATTILANA is a freelance food writer and recipe developer based in San Francisco. She is the author of *Repertoire* and writes a bimonthly cooking column for *The San Francisco Chronicle*. Her work has been featured in *TASTE*, *Saveur*, and *Martha Stewart Living*.

JOHN BIRDSALL is a James Beard Award–winning writer based in Oakland, California, and former cook of seventeen years. His writing has appeared in such publications as *Bon Appétit*, *Eater*, and *Food & Wine*.

JONATHAN MELENDEZ is a L.A.-based cookbook author, blogger, recipe developer, and food photographer. He photographs regularly for such food sites as *Joy the Baker*, Food.com, and *Go Bold with Butter*.

JOSIE SMITH-MALAVE is the chef and co-owner of Bubbles + Pearls in Wilton Manors, Florida, and was a contestant on Season 2 of *Top Chef*.

JULIA TURSHEN is the bestselling author of numerous cookbooks, including *Now & Again* and *Feed the Resistance*, and is the founder of Equity at the Table, an inclusive digital directory of women and nonbinary professionals in the food industry.

JUSTIN BURKE-SAMSON is the co-owner of Bonjour Y'all in Davidson, North Carolina, the former pastry chef for Kindred, and a freelance food writer. His writing has been featured in a number of publications, such as *Eater* and *Compound Butter*.

JUSTIN CHAPPLE is the culinary director-at-large for *Food & Wine*, host of the James Beard–nominated online video series *Mad Genius Tips*, and author of *Just Cook It! 145 Built-to-Be-Easy Recipes That Are Totally Delicious*.

KAREN AKUNOWICZ is the chef and owner of Fox & the Knife in Boston, and was a contestant on Season 13 of *Top Chef*. She received the James Beard Foundation's Best Chef of the Northeast award in 2018.

KATY SMITH is the executive chef for QDOBA and former executive creative chef for Puesto. She worked as Rick Bayless's right-hand person, acting as a culinary producer for the Emmy–winning PBS show *Mexico: One Plate at a Time* and the James Beard Award–winning podcast *The Feed*.

KIA DAMON is a freelance chef, the culinary director for Cherry Bombe, and the former head chef of Lalito in New York City.

KRISTOPHER EDELEN is the chef and founder of HOTPANnyc, a culinary events company based in New York. He has been a contestant on *Chopped* and *Cutthroat Kitchen* and featured in *First We Feast*.

LIBBY WILLIS & BILL CLARK are the co-owners of MeMe's Diner in Brooklyn, an inclusive diner the duo has described as being "very, very gay." In 2019 Willis was named one of *Eater*'s Young Guns.

LIZ ALPERN is the co-owner of The Gefilteria and author of *The Gefilte Manifesto*. She is the founder of Queer Soup Night, a party with soup and community at its center. In 2014 she was named to *Forbes*' 30 Under 30 for Food & Drink.

LUKAS VOLGER is the cofounder and editorial director of *Jarry*, a biannual food magazine with a focus on queer culture. He is the author of several cookbooks, including *Bowl: Vegetarian Recipes for Ramen, Pho, Bibimbap, Dumplings, and Other One-Dish Meals*.

MELISSA KING is a chef ambassador for Whole Foods and was a finalist on Season 12 of *Top Chef*.

MICHAEL MARINO & JORGE MORET are the co-owners of City Saucery, an artisan, small-batch tomato sauce and condiment company based in Brooklyn.

NATASHA CASE & FREYA ESTRELLER are the cofounders of Coolhaus, an ice cream company creating premium cookie sandwiches, pints, and bars based in Culver City, California. Case has been named to *Forbes*' 30 Under 30 for Food & Drink and a *Zagat* 30 Under 30.

NIK SHARMA is a columnist for *The San Francisco Chronicle*, founder of the popular food blog *A Brown Table*, and author of the James Beard Award–nominated cookbook *Season: Big Flavors, Beautiful Food*.

OLLIE WALLECK is the executive chef of the Broken Shaker and Café Integral at Freehand Chicago.

ORLANDO SOTO is the pastry chef for Catch Steak in New York City and the former executive pastry chef of Ilili.

PICHET ONG is a pastry chef and author of *The Sweet Spot: Asian-Inspired Desserts*. He has worked at several renowned restaurants, including Chez Panisse, Spice Market, and Jean-Georges, and has been nominated for a James Beard Foundation Outstanding Pastry Chef award two times.

PREETI MISTRY is a chef and author of *The Juhu Beach Club Cookbook: Indian Spice, Oakland Soul*. She has been nominated for a James Beard Foundation Best Chef of the West award two times and was a contestant on Season 6 of *Top Chef*.

REBEKAH PEPPLER is a Los Angeles– and Paris-based writer, food stylist, and author of the James Beard Award–nominated *Apéritif: Cocktail Hour the French Way*. Her work has been featured in such publications as *Saveur*, *Epicurious*, and *The New York Times*.

RICK MARTINEZ is a freelance food writer and recipe developer based in New York. He is a contributing senior food editor for *Bon Appétit* and has had work published in *Food Network*, *Food & Wine*, and *Epicurious*.

RITA SODI & JODY WILLIAMS are the chefs and co-owners of Via Carota. In 2019 they won the James Beard Foundation's award for Best New Chef: New York City.

RUBY TANDOH is a food writer and author of three books, including *Eat Up!: Food, Appetite and Eating What You Want*. She was a runner-up on Season 4 of *The Great British Bake Off* and has written for several publications, including *The Guardian*, *Vice*, and *Elle*.

RYAN ALVAREZ & ADAM MERRIN are food bloggers based in Eagle Rock, California, and authors of *Husbands That Cook: More Than 120 Irresistible Vegetarian Recipes and Tales from Our Tiny Kitchen*.

SANA JAVERI KADRI is the founder of Diaspora Co., a queer woman of color–owned spice business based in Oakland, California, which aims to put money, equity, and power into the hands of Indian farmers.

SARAH KIRNON is the chef and owner of Miss Ollie's Caribbean restaurant in Oakland, California.

SEAN DOOLEY is a New York–based food and lifestyle stylist. His work has been featured in several publications, including *Bon Appétit*, *Cherry Bombe*, and *Epicurious*.

SUSAN FENIGER is the co-chef and co-owner of Border Grill—a small restaurant chain located in Los Angeles and Las Vegas—and author of multiple cookbooks. She has been featured on several television shows, including *Top Chef Masters*, and was inducted into the James Beard Foundation's Who's Who of Food & Beverage in America in 1985.

TED ALLEN is the host of Food Network's *Chopped* and author of *In My Kitchen: 100 Recipes and Discoveries for Passionate Cooks* and *The Food You Want to Eat: 100 Smart, Simple Recipes*. He was the food and wine expert on *Queer Eye for the Straight Guy* and is the recipient of two James Beard Foundation awards.

TIFFANI FAISON is the owner of three restaurants in Boston (Sweet Cheeks, Tiger Mama, and Fool's Errand) and was a finalist on the first season of *Top Chef*. She was nominated for the James Beard Foundation's Best Chef of the Northeast award in 2019.

VAUGHN VREELAND is a senior video journalist for *New York Times Cooking*. Previously he was a producer and onscreen personality for *Tasty*.

VIRGINIA WILLIS is a chef and author of six cookbooks, including *Lighten Up, Y'all: Classic Southern Recipes Made Healthy and Wholesome*. She splits her time between Atlanta, Georgia, and Hatfield, Massachusetts.

VON DIAZ is a New York–based radio producer and food writer, and the author of *Coconuts and Collards: Recipes and Stories from Puerto Rico to the Deep South*.

WOLDY A. REYES is the chef and founder of Woldy Kusina, a boutique catering company based in New York that has been featured in *Goop* and *New York* magazine.

YOTAM OTTOLENGHI is a James Beard Award–winning author of several cookbooks, including *Ottolenghi Simple* and *Plenty: Vibrant Vegetable Recipes from London's Ottolenghi*, and is the co-owner of multiple restaurants throughout London.

ZAC YOUNG is the pastry director of Craveable Hospitality Group in New York City and has appeared in numerous television shows, including *Unique Sweets* and *Top Chef: Just Desserts*.

Index